How to
Single Parent

How to Single Parent

Dr. Fitzhugh Dodson

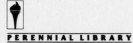

PERENNIAL LIBRARY

Harper & Row, Publishers, New York
Cambridge, Philadelphia, San Francisco, Washington
London, Mexico City, São Paulo, Singapore, Sydney

A hardcover edition of this book is published by Harper & Row, Publishers, Inc.

First PERENNIAL LIBRARY edition published 1988

Designed by Erich Hobbing

Library of Congress Cataloging-in-Publication Data

Dodson, Fitzhugh, 1923–
    How to single parent.

    "Perennial Library."
    l. Single parents—United States.   2. Children of single parents—United States.   3. Child psychology.
I. Title.
HQ759.915.D63   1988   306.8'56   86-46057
ISBN 0-06-091487-4 (pbk.)

88 89 90 91 92 FG 10 9 8 7 6 5 4 3 2 1

DEC   '88

To Jenny, my freelance editor, who has edited eight books of mine—a wise and delightful woman who has taught me how to shorten twenty-six-word sentences to nineteen-word sentences

Contents

Single Parenting

1. Who Is the Single Parent?

A lot of people think a single parent is a mother who works because she has to and takes care of her children because that's her mission in life.

But I object to defining a single parent as a mother whose life is confined to working and raising her children. It is as much a mistake for the single parent as it is for the parents of an intact family to totally center their lives around the raising of their children. As a general guideline, the first priority of the family should be the relationship of husband and wife. The second priority is the raising of the children. Of course, the younger the children are, the more protection and care they require. And all children require ongoing love and guidance. But if the parents devote themselves exclusively to their children, the marital relationship will sooner or later deteriorate and with it the emotional lives of the children.

The same guidelines apply to the single parent. Her first priority should be parenting *herself* as a person, and this includes having a satisfying social life. If she devotes her whole life, apart from her work, to her children, she is not doing them any favors.

Incidentally, I speak of the single parent as a mother because this is usually the case. Statistics show that there are far more widows than there are widowers with young children. And about 95 percent of divorced parents with custody are mothers. It's also unfortunately true that single fathers without custody often take a very passive and inactive role in the raising of their children.

As I was saying, the mother who devotes her life totally to her children is not doing them any favors. For it is not an *abundance* of attention that children need; they need *quality* attention. And quality attention comes from a parent who is reasonably happy and satisfied with her own life. The mother who continually sacrifices herself for her children will sooner or later build up a subconscious hostility to them which will undermine her relationship to them. Also, this kind of sacrificing becomes burdensome to the children.

A twelve-year-old I know finally said to his mother, "Mom, why don't you go out on dates like other single mothers do?" He was expressing a perfectly natural feeling for a child in his position. He was feeling the weight of his mother's overconcern for him as oppressive, cloying, and smothering. He wanted her to leave him alone for a bit and devote herself to something else besides him.

Often the self-sacrificing mother imagines that her children are someday going to be very grateful for all she has done for them. But she is likely to be disappointed. I once had a patient, a forty-two-year-old single mother, with four children ranging in age from nine to eighteen. In the first years following the divorce she had really devoted herself to those children. She had turned down invitations for parties and other events she would dearly have loved to go to. She had dated very little, even though she was an attractive woman, because she felt that time spent in dating was time robbed from her children. She was sure that the children were really grateful for the attention she lavished on them.

In this woman's therapy sessions I had been trying to get her to see that she had gotten some of her priorities backward. Then came Mother's Day of the year her eldest turned nineteen. As she recounted the story, she was alternately crying and expressing intense anger.

She said that all day long on Mother's Day she had anticipated that the children had a surprise for her, since they were acting as if it were just an ordinary Sunday like any other. So she waited and waited. As the children went about their own fun all day, eating the meals she fixed and dashing away again, she began to face the reality that there was to be no surprise. In fact, she reluctantly came to the conclusion that the children had forgotten it was Mother's Day.

Finally, at dinner she said something to them. They all acted chagrined and said they had simply forgotten. The mother was crying and furious. "After all the things I do for

you all year and all the sacrifices I make, you can't even remember to wish me a happy Mother's Day or give me a card.
God forbid you should go to the trouble of getting me a gift!"
She stamped out of the house to a neighbor's to let off steam,
leaving the dinner dishes for the children. When she came
back in about an hour, the kitchen was spick-and-span and the
children had written her a letter of apology, telling her what
chores they would do that week to make up for Mother's Day.
But the mother had learned a lot from this episode. She told
me, "From now on I'm going to stop living for my children
and begin living for me!"

And that is the philosophy, dear single mother, that I hope
you will live by also—not in any way neglecting your children,
of course, but making sure that you are taking care of yourself
too. That is why, in this book, I am going to talk to you not
only as a parenter of your children. We will discuss the full
spectrum of your life: as a woman, as a parent, as a woman
who probably works outside the home, as a woman who is
under incredible time pressure, as an adult with friends of
your own, as a lover, and as a possible wife to a new man. You
are all of these things, and to leave out any one of them is to
do you an injustice.

In my other books I have pointed out to the mother in an
intact family that she needs to learn two very complex skills
in order to raise her children successfully. First, she needs to
learn child psychology, especially the eight psychological
stages from birth through adolescence. She also needs to
learn the teaching strategies by which she can teach her children acceptable behavior and discourage them from unacceptable behavior.

But when a mother leaves an intact home and becomes a
single parent, not only do some of her everyday management
skills become more important, but she must learn some new
and complex social skills as well. She needs to learn, if she
does not already know, how to master time rather than having
time master her. What with working, taking care of the children, managing a home, and the other things she needs to do,
it is even harder than before for her to master time. That is
why there is a chapter in this book called "You: Manager of
Your Time."

This newly single woman must also learn some complex and vital social skills. For example, she may think she knows how to attract men, but in many cases this is an illusion. Many women don't even know how to talk to the men they are dating. And that is why there are two chapters in this book: "How to Find a Good Man" and "Men, Dating, Sex, and Marriage."

The single parent also needs to learn certain other new skills because she no longer has a spouse with whom to talk over the raising of the children. These new skills have to do with how you handle children when you are 100 percent responsible for their raising.

You might sum up all of these statements by saying that a single mother must be an incredibly skilled juggler. She juggles her work, her children, her friends, any outside activities, and her dating. As a single parent once said to me, "Just as I learn to juggle four balls, someone always throws me another!" This book will cover all of the varied components of single parenting. And it will discuss how you can improve your handling of each area.

Let me state frankly my view of the single parent's life. Some women feel they are stuck with being single until their children have grown up. Others proclaim emphatically that they never want to get married again. They say, "My last marriage was the biggest trauma of my life. Get married again? You think I'm crazy?"

Certainly any woman is entitled to her own feelings about remarriage. But I think it is only fair for me to state my position on this: I think it is much more difficult to be a successful single parent than a successful parent in an intact family. But as I will show you, there are many ways in which you can make single parenting easier on yourself and your children. And I am certainly not in favor of your rushing into marriage with some inadequate male just because you want to go back to having a new intact family.

But I view the single-parent family as a transition stage—a transition from the breakup of the old unsuccessful family to a new family that is going to work. I think if you can establish a relationship with a good partner and create a warm and loving new family, both you and your children are going to be better off. So that's the point of view from which this book is written. If you have no interest in marrying again, then simply skip the few chapters that deal with that subject. But if you are interested in marrying and establishing a new family, then by all means read with tender loving care the chapters on that subject.

2. Is There Life Beyond Divorce and Widowhood?

Yes! There emphatically is life beyond divorce and widowhood!

When I think of this question it reminds me of the joke about the old farmer. A man asked him, "Zeke, do you believe in baptism?"

"Believe in it? Why, I've seen it done!"

Yes, I believe there is happy and vital life beyond widowhood and divorce because I see it happen all the time. And in some cases in my work as a psychologist and counselor, I have helped it happen.

I remember a forty-two-year-old widow who came to see me several years ago. She had been happily married for thirteen years. Then her husband suddenly died of a heart attack. She was desolate. We spent approximately seven months discussing her grief. Then one morning she came in and opened the session by announcing, "Dr. Dodson, I think I need some men in my life." I said, "It looks like your grief work is coming to a close." She agreed that it was.

I discussed with her the various ways she could meet single men. One of the options we settled on was a well-known singles magazine in which people place ads anonymously, under a code number. I helped her compose her first ad. It drew about eighty responses. She brought them in to talk over with me and decide which ones to answer first. Her first seven dates were nice men, but they didn't strike any fire with her.

But her eighth date, an associate professor of philosophy at UCLA, definitely did strike fire! They were quite strongly attracted to one another and she put the other responses to her ads on the shelf. In a little over a year they were married.

Does that sound like a success story? It is. This was a

woman who did the grief work that was necessary to mourn the catastrophic end of her happy marriage. But once she had done that work, she set about steadfastly to find a man and create a new family for herself and her children. She had two late teenagers, boys sixteen and eighteen. At first they were somewhat jealous of their stepfather-to-be. But with some guidance, they were able to get their feelings out in the open and work on them. Within six months the new family was pretty solidly established as a loving, caring group of people.

Fortunately this widow had a good marriage. We shouldn't pretend (at least to ourselves) that a marriage was a good one now that the spouse is dead. When a poor marriage ends in death, the woman may feel secretly relieved, but she may also feel guilty for having such feelings. However, feelings are only feelings, and we should not feel guilty about them. We can't control feelings, and it's damaging to a person to try to do so. We can control our actions, however, and if we had wished somebody dead and then caused it, that would be something to feel guilty about. Thoughts and feelings should be guilt-free; only actions should cause guilt.

Here's another story from my counseling files. This was a thirty-one-year-old woman with a boy of two and a girl of six. She came to see me a few months after her divorce was final. I counseled her for about a year and a half, and then she and I felt she had completed her adjustment. Four years later I got a long letter from her. I'm going to paraphrase the letter (partly to preserve the woman's privacy), but it went something like this:

Dear Dr. Dodson:

I'll bet you're surprised hearing from me after all this time. I live up in northern California now with my new husband, who is an architect. I just wanted you to know that all the things we talked about when I was seeing you have worked out beautifully. I firmed up with the children and stopped letting them push me around. I got a baby-sitter for them one day a week and told them that was Mommy's Vacation Day. They didn't care for it much at first, but they got used to it and the whole tone of my life improved!

I started going out in the evenings, just like I promised you.

One of the things I did was enroll in that photography class I'd been talking about. And that's where I met Ted, the super man I'm married to. He was taking the class because he'd always wanted to but never gotten around to it before, like me. It's a hobby we pursue together now—we take the kids on photography field trips on weekends, and things like that. Anyway, we met in that class and I was attracted to him right away. Eventually I got up the nerve to invite him to have coffee with me one night after class. That was the beginning of our big romance—which is still going on, even though we've been married nearly two years.

Just before Ted and I were married we relocated in the San Francisco area, because Ted had a great opportunity with an architectural firm here. So that's where we're living now. It's beautiful up here. We all love it. And Ted has never had children, so I'm coaching him on how to be a good parent. I give him hugs and kisses every time he finishes reading a chapter in one of your books! How's that for the positive reward system! Both of the kids like him and he spends a lot of time with them. Well, that's about all the news, and it's good. I'm really grateful for the help you gave me when I needed it. Not just for teaching me how to meet a great guy like Ted, but for teaching me how to develop the unused parts of my personality and lead a richer, fuller life. Thanks and God bless!

Vivian

This widow and this divorcée were able to get out of the slough of despond because they learned some very basic social skills that you need as a single parent. They learned how to express their feelings, both positive and negative. They learned how to parent their children by themselves, and how to nurture themselves. They learned how to attract members of the opposite sex, form an exclusive commitment, and ultimately get married. They weren't born with knowledge of these skills and school didn't teach them. They learned these things on the job as a divorcée and a widow. And you can learn them too. That's why I have written this book.

In order to learn to be self-assertive, confident, and adventurous, the first thing you have to do is to cast off a number of myths and old wives' tales about divorce and widowhood. Myths are funny things. People believe them even though there's no scientific proof to back them up. The classic example, of course, was the belief that the sun went around the earth. Millions of people believed that until it was finally demolished by scientific evidence. But there are still plenty of myths and folktales that people continue to believe even though they're simply not true. Here are some of them.

Myth No. 1: Broken homes produce psychologically maladjusted children. There is no scientific evidence for this whatsoever. As a matter of fact, various studies have shown that intact homes produce a higher percentage of maladjusted kids than broken homes do.

You run into the term *broken home* everywhere, and I wish it had never been invented. I often hear it in meetings with teachers and school administrators when we are having a psychological conference about a child. If the child is from a divorced family, almost certainly someone will say, in a tone of voice that implies the whole problem has been solved, "Well, of course, Harry comes from a broken home." If we later discuss another child whose family happens to be intact but is having the same problems of disrupting the class, I am gravely tempted to say (but I don't), "Well, of course, Egbert comes from an intact home."

You read the same kind of thing in the newspaper sometimes, when somebody writes about a correlation between declining test scores and other measures of academic performance and an increase in divorce. I would nominate this kind of discussion for the Foggy Thinking Award. If divorce in fact causes declining test scores and poor academic performance, then what about the children who are from intact families? What causes their declining test scores and poor academic performance?

Myth No. 2: Divorce means you are a failure. In my work as a counselor, I have heard divorced women say that about themselves for many years. They cry and say, "I'm just a failure. That's all I am, a failure." Now, many of these people have at one time or another left jobs they were unhappy in because of bosses or something else and taken new jobs. But they didn't label themselves failures for doing that. So why do they label themselves failures for leaving one unwanted partner and ultimately finding a new partner? Because society does not put a heavy moral burden on changing jobs. Society does not tell us we are immoral creatures or failures if we change jobs. But society does tell us this if we decide to leave an unsatisfactory marriage and ultimately find a new one.

Myth No. 3: Once you have been divorced you are doomed to keep repeating yourself by marrying the same type of husband you married before. Once again, there is no scientific evidence for this, but a lot of people seem to believe it. I have heard it in many places. The only one I have observed who may fit this description is the woman who divorces an alcoholic only to marry another alcoholic. But even here there are many exceptions.

In general, there is no evidence to back up this idea that you unconsciously seek out the same type of man as the old husband you just divorced. I have a friend who has been married three times. She gets a big laugh out of this idea of marrying the same man each time. She says her three husbands are as different as her three children. I can vouch for the truth of that. And I am happy to report that this third marriage appears to be the best one.

Myth No. 4: If you are a parent raising children by yourself, you are at a huge disadvantage compared with a mother in an intact family. I don't think this is true at all. As I have pointed out, to be a good parent you need to learn two complex skills. One is child psychology, especially the psychology of the different stages from birth through adolescence. The second is the skills with which to teach your child acceptable behavior while avoiding unacceptable behavior.

I would guess that no more than 10 percent of America's parents in intact homes have more than the haziest notion of either of these two complex skills. The only philosophy a lot of parents know about raising children is Yell and Swat. It is a grievous error to imagine there is wise and wonderful child raising going on in all the intact families in America, with single parents being left far behind. Bah and humbug! If you are a single parent who takes the time and effort to learn the skills of parenting, and in addition the special skills you need as a single parent, you will undoubtedly end up doing a far better job of parenting than most parents in intact families. Myth No. 5: Widows are sexless and reclusive. People don't usually state it that bluntly, but that is the implication. I do know widows who are sexless (as far as I can tell), and some who don't seem interested in keeping a social network going. But then I know some divorced and nondivorced women who are like that too. So where does that leave us? All things considered, I don't think widows are any more sexless or reclusive than any other group. And yet this myth persists.

I recently ran across a book on widowhood that actually used this as a subtitle: "A new and creative approach to being alone." Can you imagine that? Here is the author of an entire book for widows, telling them that all they have to look forward to in life is being alone. This same book mentions that celibacy is a time-honored stance for single persons and that celibacy in later years is a perfectly acceptable life-style. I disagree emphatically. I think celibacy is a highly negative life-style, and I think we do widows a disservice by telling them that we expect them to live a quiet, respectable, and stagnant life by themselves. So if you are a sexy widow, full of high spirits and joie de vivre, just go your own merry way, attracting charming men, and pay no attention to people who say you should live some other way.

I am sure some of you reading this have been affected by one or more of these myths. Throw off any of these myths or old wives' tales that may be preventing you to some extent from becoming the zesty, adventuresome, self-confident person you really are.

3. How to Survive in the Divorce Jungle

Suppose you are flying down to Rio de Janeiro in Brazil. But on the way, your plane crashes in the Amazon jungle, the Mato Grosso. You are the only survivor. The plane is totaled and all the other people are dead. You are in a state of utter psychological shock.

You have never in your whole life been in a place such as this. You are totally unprepared for it. You have no notion of what to do or how to survive. There are no paths through the dense undergrowth and you have no machete to chop a path for yourself. You know that there are poisonous snakes and tarantulas in the jungle, and the thought of this makes your skin crawl.

You have had no survival training of any sort. You don't know what is safe to eat. You don't know how to catch or trap animals for food. You don't know which way is out. Obviously you are not going to last long in this alien and hostile environment.

Divorce is like that awesome jungle terrain. And if you have had no divorce survival training, you are going to find the divorce jungle very similar to the Mato Grosso jungle.

Make no mistake about it, divorce is a jungle, but there is a beautiful valley on the other side of it. One of the main purposes of this book is to provide you with a reliable map as well as a survival guide for the divorce jungle, and this chapter is devoted entirely to the divorced or divorcing parent.

Divorce is one of the greatest emotional stresses you will probably ever experience, but at the same time it offers you a great opportunity, the opportunity for a new chance at happiness. We will elaborate on both of these points throughout the book.

*   *   *

Single parenting begins on the day that one parent communicates to the other, "I want a divorce."

From that day on, only one of two things can happen: Either both parents end up agreeing to the divorce, or both parents, no matter how unhappy they are, band together to seek professional counseling to work out their difficulties and restore the marriage to health. I would certainly recommend the second course to any couple, although very few avail themselves of it. Even if the couple have to borrow money for the counseling, it is by far the smartest thing they can do.

Counseling is a no-lose situation. If it succeeds in helping the partners work out the trouble spots in their relationship and puts joy back in their marriage, that is certainly a "win." But even if they learn through counseling that they are unable to restore their relationship to effective and happy functioning, they have gained something valuable from the counseling. Instead of going through the divorce process as a bloody, vicious battle, the counseled couple may have been able to get some of the anger out of their systems and be able to work together in handling the children. Although they may end up divorced from each other, they can never divorce themselves from their children.

As to what causes divorce, I think it is fruitless to speculate. If you have a thousand divorces, you have a thousand different reasons and sets of circumstances. Some marriages break up apparently because of sexual problems. In other marriages the couple have great sexual compatability, but that doesn't prevent a divorce from happening. Some divorces are mulled over for years before one of the partners finally brings it up. Other divorces are quite impulsive. With some divorces there is "another woman" or "another man." With others there is no such animal. What I am saying is that there are so many permutations and combinations of personality factors which lead to a breakup that it is futile to try to figure out what "caused" a divorce. And most of the real causes are buried in the husband's and wife's unconscious minds anyway, where they can only be gotten out by psychotherapy.

So let's go back to the point in time where one of the couple broaches the idea of divorce to the other. Let's suppose it is the woman who has brought up the subject to her husband.

Chances are she has not consulted a lawyer before she brings the subject up. In my twenty years' experience with patients, I have not met one who consulted a lawyer first. I think this is a mistake.

Why should both husband and wife see a lawyer as soon as possible if they have decided against counseling? To find out where they stand legally. For there are many legal aspects of the divorce process of which most people are totally ignorant, and they should not start out through the jungle without legal advice.

But now we come to a very sticky and difficult question: How are they going to find a good lawyer?

My personal unscientific guess is that no more than 25 percent of the lawyers in the United States are intelligent, competent, and honest. Former Supreme Court Chief Justice Warren Burger has gone on record saying that 50 percent of the trial lawyers of America are incompetent. Personally, I think his figures are low.

So how are you going to find a good lawyer? Let's begin by looking at how most people find a lawyer. They have one recommended to them by a friend, or a doctor or dentist or some other professional. They stick with that lawyer if he is good, or when they find out how bad he is they change to another one. But by that time the damage is usually done.

Instead, I suggest you get recommendations for *three* different lawyers and arrange an interview with each to evaluate them. Naturally, you don't tell them about the others or that *you* are interviewing them. Ask them to tell you in one hour the important things they feel you ought to know and do in getting this divorce. I think you will be able to tell from the "vibes" you get which lawyer you want to hire. Of course you pay each of them their customary fee for the hour's consultation.

Choosing a lawyer will certainly be one of the most important things you do in the whole process of the divorce. And here is another reason why I believe your choice of lawyer is so important. My state of California has a no-fault divorce law, which means that the court does not attempt to judge who is "at fault" for the divorce. Instead, they are simply supposed to divide the property fifty-fifty. In the years since we have had this law, I have yet to hear of a divorce in which things were in reality divided fifty-fifty. In each divorce I have observed, the person with the smartest lawyer has gotten the larger division of the community property. Do I need to say more?

Not only should your lawyer be intelligent, competent, and honest, but he or she should be a lawyer who negotiates with the other party wherever possible rather than go to court. The reason for this is simple. As a lawyer friend of mine said, "If I negotiate the divorce settlement (or any other settlement, for that matter) outside of court, you may not like all of what is decided, but at least you know in advance exactly what you are willing to settle for. But if it goes to a judge to decide, who knows what you will get?" Who knows what goes on in the head of a judge? Your jaw would drop with astonishment if you could hear some judges' comments and decisions.

For example, one patient of mine, a father, reported this amazing experience. He and his ex-wife had worked out a visitation schedule for their two young children, six and ten. The father was to have visitation on Tuesdays to take them for dinner, on Fridays to take them to the movies, and every other weekend. Later, the mother got angry at him and took him to court to cut down the visitation. He was a good and loving father, with no alcoholic or other emotional problems which would justify having his visitation cut down.

The judge arbitrarily cut out the Tuesday and Friday visitations. His lawyer interceded and asked permission from the judge to hear the father's side. The father told of the importance of those two visits to the father-son relationships, to which the judge replied, "Tuesday and Friday are too much. I'll give you your choice of one." The father chose Friday, but told me that he could hardly believe what he had heard. How could two evenings a week be too much? Too much for what? How could the children possibly be harmed by two evenings a week (and one of them a dinner!)? Where did the judge get those strange ideas?

Here's another scene. I was an expert witness in this case. The mother suspected the father was poisoning the minds of the children, aged eight and ten, against her during his every-other-weekend visitation. The mother asked me to do a thorough psychological evaluation and clinical interview with the children. I did that, spending five hours with each child. The results were clear-cut: The father *was* systematically poisoning the minds of the children against their mother. The mother wanted the court either to order him to cease and desist, or to not allow him to visit the children, or at the least to cut his visitation down.

In court, the judge called the father and his lawyer and the mother and her lawyer up to the front of the court. The judge addressed the two lawyers. "Have you gentlemen got anything new since the last court appearance?"

"No," said the father's lawyer.

"Yes, Your Honor," said the mother's lawyer. "We have a report by a child psychologist based upon five hours of testing and interviewing with each child. The report finds evidence that the father has been systematically and willfully poisoning the minds of the children against the mother."

"Is that all?" asked the judge.

"Yes, Your Honor."

"You shouldn't have bothered the court's time with something so meaningless as this. Case dismissed."

Can you imagine such a thing? A ten-year-old child would have more sense than the judge. And these examples could be multiplied a hundredfold. So you can see why, as a rule of thumb, I believe it is better to negotiate with the opposite party than to leave it up to a judge. Negotiation will also save you a great deal of money in legal expenses. Court time, especially in a contested case, can seem to run on forever, and the costs can be enormous. And at least some of those expenses are likely to be paid out of your mutual coffers.

Remember that *everything* you and your spouse can work out between you not only saves lawyer money but gets you more of what you want. Of course you may be so hostile to one another you can't manage to work out everything between you. Well, that's one of the things we have lawyers for.

Ask your lawyer to submit a monthly bill with an account of just what he did for you and how long he spent doing it. Otherwise I guarantee you'll be stunned by the amount of his final bill (with just the money stated but no indication of what he did and how much time he spent doing it).

Sooner or later, you and your spouse are going to have to

divide up all of your property between you. Some of that may be so complicated you need the help of lawyers or accountants. But just between the two of you you should be able to divide up other things such as books, phonograph records and tapes, tools, furniture, art, and cars.

WARNING! Once you have divided these things, each of you should take your portions to your own residences. Don't leave all of the divided portion with one spouse. Your spouse may ordinarily be an honest, warmhearted, easygoing person. But during the divorce he may turn into a cobra. Here are only two examples out of many I could give.

During the process of his divorce, my dentist was vacationing in Florida. He got a phone call from a friend of his telling him that his wife was having a garage sale and selling off the furnishings of the house. He phoned her. "Me sell the house furnishings? Don't be silly. I wouldn't do a thing like that. I'm just getting rid of a few old things I don't want. Trust me."

When he got back to Los Angeles he found the house completely empty! She had gutted it at the garage sale, sold all the furnishings, and moved to San Francisco.

Here's another one. A divorcing couple who were selling their house had 152 art objects to divide up: paintings, mobiles, small sculptures. The husband said he had lots of storage space in his new apartment, so the wife let him take the artworks temporarily. As part of the divorce agreement in court they agreed to set no value on anything but simply to alternate in choosing which art objects they wanted. This sounded fair to the wife until the evening that the couple and their lawyers met at the husband's apartment to actually divide the art. The husband (the cobra) informed the wife that 124 of the artworks had mysteriously disappeared! She was furious, but her lawyer told her there was nothing she could do about it. If she tried to do something it would cost much more in lawyer's fees than the value of the art. So she gritted her teeth and divided up the remaining 28 art objects.

Remember the old saying, "Possession is nine tenths of the law," and don't give up possession of anything to your spouse until the judge has awarded it to him.

Most people are totally unprepared for what they encounter in the divorce courtroom. You will no doubt hear a good deal of lying when you are there. A judge once called both divorce lawyers into his chambers to discuss an important point. After their brief discussion, the judge said, "Well, gentlemen, should we go back into the court and hear some more perjury?" But don't let this tempt you to indulge in some lying of your own. Stick to the truth. It's better by far for you in the long run. Just don't think of the courtroom as a place that is anchored in reality. Instead, think of it as a kind of never-never land, where you will hear strange and wonderful pronouncements from lawyers and judges and spouses.

I can't impress upon you too strongly how crucial the judge's decisions are to the rest of your life with your children. Once he has laid out the division of property, the custody, the child visitation, the child support, or the alimony, it's as if his rulings are carved in stone. So you want to do everything you can to make sure these decisions are ones you approve of. As the years go on, you will have a terrible time changing them.

And remember this: A judge does not have to give any reason for his decisions. And a judge cannot be sued. His rulings are the closest things to the Ten Commandments, carved on stone tablets, that we have in our society.

Your attorney may say to you, "Oh, don't worry, we can always appeal this decision of the court." What you don't know is that the only sure thing about appealing a ruling to a higher court is that it will cost you a lot more in lawyer's fees. And you should know that only about 1 percent of divorce court appeals are successful.

Now that I've given you some information about how to survive in the divorce jungle, I want to turn to a very important topic: how to break the news to your children. This next chapter applies both to you and to the parent who must tell her children about the death of their other parent.

4. How to Tell Your Children

Telling your children about a divorce or the death of a parent is a difficult task indeed. Your children may at first be almost as concerned about your emotional state as about the news you bring them. For they love you, and your hurt concerns them greatly. They also have probably never seen you emotionally out of control, and this may alarm them. So you need to do your best to comfort the children and reassure them that your life and theirs will continue in a stable, constant, and loving way.

Telling Your Children About the Divorce

The situations of divorce and death are so different that we need to talk about them separately. So first, let's discuss how to tell your children about a separation and divorce.

No matter how difficult the home atmosphere has been before a divorce, the children will be upset and angry about the departure of a parent. If the parent has been abusive, the children may have relief mixed in with other feelings. But the loss of a parent is a sad and angry time for the children, even though they may manage to cover up their feelings. And remember that the children will be much more upset or angry if you try to avoid telling them, or tell them in a way that does not take their feelings into account.

I think it is much better if both parents tell the children about the coming separation. Although the news is unpleasant, at least the children will feel that their parents are united in telling them. If one parent makes up an excuse to get out of talking to the children, then of course the other parent has no alternative but to talk to the children herself. If you are the one left to do this, simply say, "Your father was too upset to tell you, so that's why I'm telling you by myself." This is probably a truthful description of the situation, whether or not it seems like it to you at the moment.

In talking to the children, you need to use a slightly changed version of the formula used in court. "Do you swear to tell the truth, the whole truth, and nothing but the truth?" I advise you to tell the truth and nothing but the truth, but you do not need to tell the whole truth. For example, you do not need to explain the intimate details of your sexual relationship, or tell incidents of a personal nature that involve a neighbor known to the children.

I always advise parents never to lie to their children about anything, whether the home is intact or single-parented. If a child is asking questions that the parent doesn't want to answer, she should simply say that the matter is personal or confidential, and she doesn't wish to discuss it. With a divorce, there may be many things you are tempted not to tell the truth about. But whatever comes up, now or later, where you don't know what to say, tell the truth—or at least as much of the truth as seems appropriate. The truth is your greatest ally in handling difficult situations with your children. And if the children catch you lying, you have lost your credibility with them. And that's a terrible thing to lose.

Should you tell all the children together about the separation, or should you divide them up according to their ages? The answer is clear-cut and definite: Tell them all together! If you divide them up according to age because their powers of comprehension depend on their ages, the ones who are told last will be very suspicious and think that things are being said behind their backs. Of course the younger ones, the twos and threes and such, will understand what is being said only on a very primitive level, and certain things will go over their heads.

If you tell all the children together, the siblings can be of emotional support to one another. Here is what one woman recalled about her parents' divorce:

"Dad was gone and Mom was upset a lot—too upset to pay much attention to us. I was only five. If it hadn't been for my eight-year-old brother I would have been lost. He kind of fathered me, I guess. And even though I was younger, I kind of took care of him too—listening to his problems, cheering him up. I remember, he even used to tell me bedtime stories." (Judith Wallerstein and Joan Kelly, *Surviving the Breakup,* New York: Basic Books, 1980)

When a parent is leaving the marriage, how far ahead of time should the children be told? Some parents wait till the very last minute, while Father is packing his bags and getting ready to dash out the door to his new apartment. The reason the parents give each other for doing this is that the children will be upset, and the sooner they get the departure over with, the easier it will be on the children. This of course is not true. The parents are attempting to protect themselves rather than the children.

Children need time to mull over and digest such a difficult message. A rule of thumb would be two or three weeks before the parent moves out. This was they are still in contact with both parents for several weeks after the crucial message has been communicated.

Parents should be sure to tell the children only when a definite decision has been made. Nothing could be more demoralizing to the children than to try to adjust to parents who are acting like yo-yos: "Yes, the divorce is on." "No, the divorce is off." "Yes, it's on again."

I'd like to elaborate now on what I said earlier about telling the children the truth. It's natural in some situations for the initiator of the divorce to want to withhold his or her identity from the children. He's afraid if the children know who wanted the divorce he will immediately be cast in the role of Bad Guy. So he tries to give the children the impression that both parents mutually wanted to separate. But that won't wash. The children will very quickly figure out who wanted the divorce and who didn't. So it's much better to tell them the truth, even if he goes through a temporary period of being labeled Mr. Bad Guy (or Mrs. Bad Guy). Only the truth will guarantee the credibility of the parents.

It's also important for the other parent to guard against playing the role of either Ms. (or Mr.) Innocent or Martyr. They may be tempting roles to play, but both of them tend to cast one parent as good and the other as bad, which is definitely not beneficial for the children's emotional welfare.

I have already said that the parents don't need to go into the details of personal things in telling the children. On the other hand, there are certain basic facts in a divorce that need to be brought out eventually. If Father has been having an affair and that has been the basic "trigger" for the divorce, you can't simply ignore that. The children will discover it quickly from many nuances of your and their father's behavior. So it's better to say, "When we were married, Father and I were in love. But now he's not in love with me anymore. He's in love with another woman, and we're not going to live together anymore." You may want to split that message up, so that first you communicate the fact that Daddy doesn't love Mommy anymore. And then when talking about it later, when the children will probably be asking questions, you can tell them that he does love someone else.

It's much better to tell your children these things than to let them hear it from other people or guess it from your behavior. If your children have to learn such facts from others or through guesswork, they then perceive their parents as withholding vital information from them. The truth may hurt them, but it won't hurt anywhere near as much as believing you have deceived them. And if the children perceive that there's something wrong but they don't know what it is because no one has told them, this will be extremely upsetting to them as well.

There is literally no problem that cannot be presented to the children in an understandable way without slinging mud at your spouse. For example: "Your father has had a problem for several years now of drinking too much. He has tried hard to control the problem but he hasn't been able to. I can't be happy living with him anymore because of this problem, so that's why I'm getting a divorce."

Even the most difficult situations can be presented truthfully and nonjudgmentally, although with care as to how much detail and the timing of it. Very young children are not going to understand certain things, and it is unwise to force unasked-for information on them that will confuse or frighten them.

Remember too that telling the children is not a one-act play which takes place once and for all the single time that you "officially" tell them. As I've said, it takes time for your children to absorb such earthshaking news. So "telling the children" is in reality a process that stretches out over a period of time. Please do not become impatient with repetitious questions from your children. The reason for asking some of the same questions over and over is that the child is working through the separation in his mind and making it more bearable.

As a matter of fact, it is worth your while to repeat a few statements to the children several times. One such statement is that the divorce was not their fault; it was entirely due to the problems of the parents. Saying this once is not enough, because children are prone to believe they are responsible for the divorce. This doesn't mean you should go to the opposite extreme and repeat it twice a day for several weeks. But once is not enough.

It is important you make clear to your child, particularly a young child, that he or she will continue to have the necessities of life—food, shelter, and clothing—in spite of the divorce. This may seem obvious to you, but it is not necessarily obvious to a child. Much of a child's thinking is what we call "magical thinking." And since Father has disappeared somewhere, a child might think that food, shelter, and clothing will also magically disappear.

It may seem to a young child that his or her father has vanished somewhere in the sky. For that reason it's important for the father to take the children to see where he lives (or is going to live, even if he hasn't moved in) as soon as possible. This enables the children to place their father, for their minds cannot grasp such abstractions as "Your father lives in an apartment close by."

It's very important not only to tell the children about the coming separation and divorce but to give them an adequate chance to ask questions and express their emotions. And please avoid clamping a lid on their emotions by saying such things as "Big boys and girls don't cry." Encourage them to cry if they feel like it.

One question that children are bound to ask is, "Is Daddy ever coming home again?" The answer to this depends on the situation, of course. But presumably by now you feel quite certain that you are going to be raising your children alone. Be gentle but definite in telling them that you and their daddy are not going to be living together anymore.

Some of you may feel that emphasis on truth telling and getting the raw facts of the divorce out in the open, even in a gentle and loving manner, will upset the children. Yes, it will. But it will upset them far less than deceiving them or letting them have false hopes. And it will certainly upset them far less than for one parent later to use unpleasant information as blackmail. For example, if the children already know that Father is in love with another woman, then neither parent can blackmail the other by threatening to tell the children. Also, when the children already have such information, it may somewhat defuse the subject if Mother chooses to bad-mouth Father to them about it.

Probably the worst thing you can do to your children in a divorce situation (short of physical abuse) is to speak ill of the other parent to them. The children love both of you. They need to continue loving both of you. And it is very difficult for them to do this if the two of you, or even one of you, bad-mouths the other. I know how tempting this is in some instances, but please try to hold yourself in check. Imagine that each time you say something vindictive or sarcastic about your spouse you are slapping your child hard in the face. For that is what you are doing to your child emotionally. If you are tempted to say something mean about your spouse to your child, remind yourself that you're about to slap her, and this image may cause you to check your tongue.

When you are answering your children's questions about their father, remember that a perfectly acceptable answer is, "I don't know." For example, Daddy has deserted the family and has not been heard of for several months. He is still working at his same job but won't answer phone calls. Your child asks you, "Why has Daddy left?"

"I don't know."

"Where has Daddy gone?"

"I don't know."

"Why doesn't Daddy see me anymore?"

"I guess Daddy must be feeling very bad inside himself, and he can't love you right now. That's too bad, because you're a very lovable little girl." (Give her a hug.)

Telling the children in the ways we have discussed is terribly important. It sets the tone for the years of the separation and divorce. Don't underestimate its importance.

Telling the children is a continuous process over time. The children may be asking you questions about the separation and your relationship long after the actual divorce.

Telling Your Children About the Death of a Parent

The way in which you tell your children about the death of a parent will depend on whether the death has been expected because of a lengthy illness or whether it is completely unexpected, such as with an accident or sudden medical problem.

Our society shuns the reality of death in many ways. For example, we tell our children that a beloved old dog needs to be "put to sleep" by the veterinarian. It would shock people if we said the dog needed to be put to death. Our taboos against facing and talking about the realities of sex are nothing compared with our taboos about death.

You will have to have the courage to break with these cultural taboos and talk openly with your children about death.

First of all, don't try to be unemotional when you tell the children. If you cry, that's perfectly all right. Although your tears will upset the children, they can handle that better than they can handle a dry, unemotional recital of facts.

If the children's father is terminally ill but is expected to live for several months or longer, it is probably better not to tell the children, especially young children, that far in advance. If the illness begins to impair his functioning, tell them, "Daddy is very sick. He has to have lots of medicine." Wait until a month or two before the expected end before telling them that their father is dying. However, children are very tuned in to what is happening, and if they ask much earlier in time, "Is Daddy going to die?" tell them, "Yes." The older the children, the more likely they are to understand what is happening and want to know the truth.

I also want to mention that some hospitals and other organizations offer hospice services, which provide help to families with a terminally ill member. In a hospice the family members face the oncoming death openly, sharing both the sadness and the special love that can exist at a time like this. In a hospice situation, the final time the family has remaining together can become deeply meaningful.

If the parent's death is sudden and unexpected, as with a heart attack, you will have to tell the children immediately. Tell them all together, if possible. And, once again, feel free to be open with your feelings and encourage the children to express theirs. Encourage them too to ask questions, and answer any that they have.

Once the children know about their father's death, the period of grief work can begin. It's helpful for you to explain what grief work is and how it works. Tell them that during the time that the grief work lasts, they will be thinking about their father and they will be sad and unhappy that he is gone. But finally they will stop thinking about him in a sad way, and then their grief work will be done. They will still love their father and have many memories about him, but they will be ready to get on with their normal, everyday living.

Throughout the period of your children's grief work you can assist them by using the feedback technique:

Sharon: "I feel awful unhappy, Mom."

Mother: "Daddy's dead and it makes you feel very unhappy."

This lets them express their emotions while feeling loved and supported by you. Eventually, all of you will complete your grief work and be able to put more energy into your new plans for living.

One of the most important things you can do for your children is to let them participate in the family's grief. Unless they are too small to understand, take them to the ritual ceremony at the church or synagogue, or the memorial service. And share your feelings of abandonment and loneliness with them, to make it easier for them to express their feelings. Don't overwhelm them with your grief; just open the pathway for them. But if a child keeps his feelings inside instead, respect his right to do so. Perhaps he will be able to express them later.

5. Separation Shock

When my daughter Robin was sixteen she spent six weeks one summer living in Trieste, Italy, as part of her experience in the School for International Living. She lived with a family who had a daughter approximately her own age. The daughter spoke about as much English as Robin spoke Italian. And the mother and father spoke no English at all.

Robin had a rough time of it for about a month. She felt completely out of place. When the family went somewhere, such as the beach, Robin felt almost completely cut off from everyone else by the language barrier. She was experiencing what anthropologists call "culture shock." This means the shock of suddenly being thrown into a new culture that is not your own. That's how you will feel from the first day you and your husband are apart: You will have separation shock.

Separation shock affects both the divorced woman and the widow, though a widow usually suffers much greater separation shock. In this chapter, we address the problems of divorce and death separately from time to time, but the discussion essentially applies to both situations.

Separation shock begins with the realization that you no longer belong to the culture of intact families. You belong to the subculture of one-parent families. But you don't even belong to that yet. Right now you feel you belong nowhere. If your husband has died, you may feel totally alone in the world except for your children.

Old friends are often of little help to you as a newly single woman. You discover that most of your married women friends don't want to see much of you anymore. They're insecure, afraid that as a single, "available" woman you are a threat to their own marriages. You even discover there is something real to their fears, because some of the husbands may actually proposition you. While this can be somewhat reassuring to your femininity, it's also a distasteful and frightening experience. Married women may particularly avoid a newly single woman if they are having trouble in their marriages.

The upshot of all this is that you feel alone in a friendless world. You are suddenly separated from so many things that were emotionally supporting you. As a divorcée, in your state of separation shock you may even begin to miss your ex-husband. Yes, he put you down; and yes, he insulted you. And yes, he may even have run around on you. But at least, with all his faults, he was around; he was there in your life. Absurd, isn't it, to think that way? But you may find yourself thinking such crazy thoughts when your whole cultural system has been thrown off balance.

Let's look at it positively. What can you do for yourself to overcome separation shock?

The first thing you need to deal with is your relationship to yourself. For you have just come through the hurricane. And it is unreal for you to expect yourself to pick yourself up from the ground and expect to continue caring for your family as before.

As I have said, in order to be a good mother to your children you first need to learn to be a good parent to yourself. You need to take care of your own psychological wounds and injuries and get your own mental and physical well-being in shape.

Your first attention must be to your grief work. For a divorced woman this means letting yourself experience your grief for your losses. Even though you may be glad to be free of an unworkable marriage, the divorce represents a loss of the hopes and dreams you had when you first married, and a loss of all of the effort you put into making the marriage work. So you must acknowledge your angers and sorrows. Don't try to hide them from yourself; it will only delay your emotional recovery. You don't need to dwell on the unhappy feelings, but you should cry your tears. And shout your anger into the clothes closet (not in front of the kids), or use up the energy in productive physical activity, such as jogging or gardening or swimming. You may get physical benefits as well as emotional ones from using your anger in this way.

If your feelings seem too strong to deal with, get yourself some psychological counseling. Divorce is traumatic, but it needn't be a knockout punch. You can bounce back.

The widow's grief work is much more intense. And the need for doing it is urgent. This means daring to fully experience your grief and get it out of your system. Avoidance of the feelings prolongs the recovery. In 1937 a fire broke out in the Coconut Grove nightclub in Boston and six hundred people were killed. Research on the close friends and relatives who survived them showed that those who could not bear to go over the clothes or personal effects of their loved ones had trouble recovering from their grief. Those who went through the clothes and memorabilia and cried intensely as they did so finished their grief work sooner and were able to start life anew.

So don't hold your feelings in. Don't shy away from your husband's things, and don't avoid thinking and talking about him, even though the tears fall. Jesus said, "Blessed are those who mourn, for they shall be comforted." But you need to truly mourn in order to find this comfort.

In addition to your grief work, you as a widow or a divorcée must start right away to build an emotional support group for yourself. By this I mean a group of eight to ten single mothers who can meet regularly (once a week or every two weeks). The group should have no leader, no outside speakers—just a chance for all of you to talk about your difficulties in being single mothers in an emotionally supportive atmosphere. You can, if you wish, choose topics for each meeting, but don't feel you must keep strictly on that topic. You should have only two rules: Nobody is to interrupt when somebody else is talking, and nobody is to be critical of what somebody else has said.

There are several ways you can get such a group together. You can organize it out of a larger singles group you belong to, such as Parents Without Partners. Or perhaps you can find other single mothers in the PTA at your children's school. You can probably find some through your church, synagogue, or other similar organization. If you're not sure which women are single parents, ask the teacher, principal, priest, minister, rabbi, or group leader. The main requirement, besides being a single parent, is that the women be congenial.

Another way to organize a group is to put a classified ad in

your small local newspaper (not a big newspaper). The ad
could read something like this:

> Single Parents Wanted. The first meeting of a new group of
> single mothers will be held in a few weeks. If you are inter-
> ested, phone Jeanette at 463-2904 for details.

You will need to screen the women who call in order to find
eight or ten congenial ones.

After your single mothers' group has been organized, try to
organize a Mothers' Hotline. This will serve a very important
purpose: Women in your group can call each other anytime
they feel an important emotional need. This can be an ex-
traordinarily valuable aid to a member in time of crisis. You
will be surprised how important this group is to everyone as
time goes by.

There is another group you should also organize, an entirely different type of emotional support group. This one
consists solely of single fathers, with or without custody of
their children. You organize this group in the same way you
did the mothers' group, and it has the same purpose and
rules. You will find it very helpful listening to these men
because they will help you to see things from the fathers'
point of view. This will help to broaden your own viewpoint
in raising your children. This group is not to be thought of
as a source of romantic males for you but as a source of
platonic friends.

You may think it strange that I suggest you organize a
single fathers' group. In your single mothers' group and
among your friends you will probably be surrounded by
women. The single fathers' group will help you cross over
gender gaps and see the issues in divorce from a single father's point of view. You may not see the many advantages of
this until you actually experience it.

You will be tempted not to organize your two emotional
support groups. You will say to yourself, "Oh, that's a lot of
trouble. I don't need a support group. I can handle my problems by myself." The English translation of this is, "I'm
scared to do it!" Sure you are. But you need to face your fears,
overcome them, and get to work organizing your groups.

If you are divorced rather than widowed, the next important thing you need to do is to find a source of new male possibilities for romance. Even widows, at the end of their grief work, must move themselves back into this mainstream.

Finding a man with whom you want to become romantically involved is of course not easy. You will have to make your way through a lot of distinctly mediocre men before you find some good ones. Or, as I have heard single women say, "You have to kiss a lot of frogs before you find yourself a prince." And as the song goes, "A good man is hard to find." So where can you find some?

Sometimes you can meet eligible men through friends. Let all your friends know you are interested in meeting someone. Even your married friends might love to match you up at a dinner party with an eligible bachelor. Accept all of these kinds of invitations.

Many single women try singles bars, and I don't say it's impossible to find a good man there but in my opinion it's unlikely. If you happen to be built along the lines of Raquel Welch or Farrah Fawcett, you may find life very busy in the singles bar scene. But I personally think that the scene is often demeaning. And there are few things more disheartening for a woman than to sit with a girlfriend in a bar, the two of them nursing their drinks all evening, with not a single man asking them to dance. Also, the quality of contact in singles bars is often depressing. All in all, I think that singles bars should be low on your list.

Second, you can try singles organizations. Some are nationwide in scope, such as Parents Without Partners. Then there are singles groups that are confined to a particular locality, church, or synagogue. Incidentally, one of the most valuable aspects of Parents Without Partners is that they have activities that both you and your children can attend, along with single fathers and their children, activities such as camping and picnics.

You can also take evening classes in college or adult education school. Sign up for courses in which you would expect to find a preponderance of men enrolled, courses such as stock market, real estate, or woodworking. You may get lucky and find yourself in a class filled with attractive single men. Or 85 percent may be married and the others not be especially attractive. In that case, you can either drop the class or learn whatever the subject has to offer. Knowing more about investments, for example, can't hurt you.

In chapter 24, "Men, Dating, Sex, and Marriage," we'll talk more about finding and dating men. If you are already at that stage in your recovery, you'll want to turn to that chapter and read it next. But if you are still in separation shock, get to work on those support groups. And get professional counseling if you need it. The money you spend on it could be the best investment you make right now. Of course you can do your grief work all by yourself, as millions of people have done. But you can do a deeper and better job with the guidance of a professional counselor.

6. Separation Shock and Your Children

We've talked about separation shock and what it does to you, the mother, and how you can cope with it. Now let's talk about separation shock and what it does to your children and how you can help them cope with it. Although much of this chapter concerns the child of divorce, the general principles apply also to the child whose parent has died.

You will sometimes hear a divorced parent say something like this: "Oh, all three of my children took the divorce in stride. Actually, they were glad to get rid of their father." Nonsense. Empirical research does not bear out this biased statement. Research shows that *all* the children in the family are upset by the divorce in the immediate aftershock period, which may last from six months to a year or even longer.

Another finding, which we mentioned earlier, is that children keenly miss even a *bad* father. If he made life miserable for them, the young children will recast him in their minds and make him into a good father who will be loving and considerate when they see him again. If their fathers are inconsistent in their visitation or fail to show up, the children make excuses for them.

Four-year-old Bobby got dressed for his father's visit two hours ahead of time. Half an hour before his dad was to arrive, Bobby started listening and checking outside for his car. *"That's* Dad now . . . I know that's my dad." Two hours later Bobby was still checking, but more slowly, with less certainty. Finally, two and a half hours late, Bobby's dad arrived: "Let's go, Bobby!" No apologies, no explanations. (Wallerstein and Kelly, *Surviving the Breakup*)

This type of scene goes on all over the United States with

children who are frantic to see their fathers no matter how their fathers treat them. On almost any terms. Just so they can see them.

You don't need to be trained as a research scientist to figure out the impact of losing a significant person. If a divorce knocks a thirty-eight-year-old woman off her feet, do you think it's going to do any less to a little four-year-old girl? No, the loss is quite as overwhelming to the children as it is to the adults. The lives of the children are disrupted fully as much by Hurricane Divorce and Hurricane Death as are the lives of the adults and children feel all alone and frightened.

A Time of Loss

The children have lost a great deal when they have lost their intact family. The family brought comfort and structure to their lives. In a divorce, the children have partially lost their father, because he is no longer a full-time father but only a visitor. They are not aware of it immediately, but they have also partially lost the mother they once had. The postdivorce mother is not going to have anywhere near as much time or energy to spend with her children as the predivorce mother did. Nor is she going to be able to be as kind and loving, because of the stress she is living with. And these facts apply doubly to the newly widowed mother.

The children's responses to such severe losses are sadness and depression. The sadness often comes out indirectly in symptoms such as overeating, various body complaints, difficulty in sleeping, inability to play actively, and moping around.

Almost all children want the divorced family restored and will carry this fantasy with them for years. No matter how bad the marriage, the children (with the exception of adolescents) want mother and father to come back together. The intensity of this wish helps ward off the acute pain of the loss they feel at the breakup of their family and their security.

A Time of Fear

What else could the loss of the intact family be except a time of fear? Children see that their world is not as secure as they assumed it was. They know for the first time that they are vulnerable. And so their minds are suddenly filled with fears, some realistic and some unrealistic. Very young children worry about such basic things as who will feed them and who will protect them from robbers. Since one parent is gone, they naturally fear that the other will be taken away from them also.

Nine-year-old Marjorie said to her mother, "If you don't love Daddy, how can I be sure what will happen? Maybe I'm next" (Wallerstein and Kelly, *Surviving the Breakup*). The perhaps erratic visiting of a father leads many children to think that it is only a question of time until he will be taken away from them once and for all. And if Daddy goes, Mother may also desert them.

In the time of separation shock, children who are deprived of a parent are swept by fears of all sorts. And in the chapters on specific ages and stages of children's development we will discuss these fears and other feelings more extensively.

A Time of Rejection

The children's interpretation of their father's leaving the home is, "Daddy's left us. He doesn't love us anymore or he wouldn't do that." And since the parents don't have the time to spend with the children they formerly did, the children take this as further evidence of rejection. Some angry mothers intensify the children's feeling of rejection by shouting over the phone or where the children can hear her. "You left us! You don't love us anymore!" The mother is really expressing her *own* feelings, but she includes the children in her tirade because she wants to ally them with her against the father.

A Time of Loneliness

During the time of separation shock children feel that both parents are moving out of their lives. One of them is already gone. The other is preoccupied with her own problems and perhaps now working at an outside job. The child feels Mother slipping away also.

The result is that the child feels deeply lonely, experiencing the feelings expressed by the old spiritual, "Sometimes I feel like a motherless child, a long way from home." The child feels all alone in a world that does not seem to love or care for him or her.

A Time of Worry

Children worry about both their parents. They worry about their absent father, whom they see only irregularly. The younger children wonder, where does he live? Who will cook his meals for him? Will he have friends to care for him?

The older children, feeling still dependent, have their fears too. Nine-year-old Janice worried, "If my mother smokes and gets cancer what will happen to me?" (Wallerstein and Kelly, *Surviving the Breakup*). Of course all of these worries are variations on the child's basic concern: "Are Mommy and Daddy all right and can they take care of me?"

Don't try to answer each separate worry of your child. Just put your arm around him or her and say (if you can truly include the father in this statement), "I know you're worried whether Mommy and Daddy can take care of you. But we both love you and we will both take care of you, and everything's going to be all right."

A Time of Anger

During separation shock, children and teenagers experience a rise in anger and aggression, both verbal and physical. Among the youngest children there is a sharp rise in temper tantrums. Older children experience a rise in hitting and verbal outbursts of anger. The anger is directed at siblings, but above all it is directed at both parents. In part this may be due to the angry outbursts of the parents toward each other, which the children have witnessed. It is as if the children had been living in a family for some years in which such outbursts were not acceptable. Now that the parents are themselves indulging in anger the rules have changed and anger is acceptable.

At any rate, the anger among the children is there. And it is an indication of how bitter and furious they feel that their parents have let them down and broken up their secure home.

The bereaved child too will feel intense anger at his father for leaving him, just as the mother feels anger toward her dead husband. And like the mother, the older child and teenager will feel ashamed and guilty.

A Time of Conflicting Loyalties

One of the most difficult things a child of divorce must contend with is his feeling (and often the reality) that a step in the direction of one parent will be seen as a betrayal of the other parent. The child loves both parents and wants to please both. But many parents will not allow him to do this. "If you're not with me, you're against me," is the parent's message.

So what is the poor child to do? He is pulled by loyalty to both his mother and his father. So if he's nice to one parent he risks rejection and anger from the other one. In such a no-win atmosphere it is not surprising that some children line up 100 percent with one parent, in bitter anger against the other.

The answer to this is simple to state but very hard to put into practice. If parents will confine their fights to what goes on between them and leave the children out of it, they will take the children out of the no-win position they occupy. But any of you who have experienced or seen at close quarters the bitter quarrels in which parents draw in the children know how difficult it is for parents to resist the temptation to get the children to take their side.

So now you know a lot of unhappy things that are going on in the minds of your children during Separation Shock time. Fear. Rejection. Loneliness. Worry. Anger. Conflicting loyalties.

I'm sure that your natural impulse would be to put your arms around your child and say, "Don't be afraid. Don't be worried. Don't be angry. Mommy and Daddy will take care of all these bad feelings for you and get them out of your system."

But your child is going to need *time* to get rid of these feelings. And while he is getting rid of them he needs an ally to understand him and to stand by him. That ally can be you if you know how to do it.

You do it by being truthful with your child, by reassuring him, and by standing by whatever you promise. And you can especially help him by using the feedback technique we mentioned earlier. Here is another feedback example. It assumes the parents are divorced. But the technique itself would be exactly the same with a bereaved child and his feelings.

Here is how many parents try to handle their children's negative feelings *not* using the feedback technique:

Tony (age ten): "I just hate the way you and Dad are always quarreling, Mom. It just makes me sick."

Mother: "Well, we just can't help quarreling sometimes when we're going through a divorce. And anyway, your father is so unreasonable, he'd make anybody quarrel."

Tony: "There you go again—you're always saying bad things about my dad. After all, he is my dad, you know."

Mother: "Every time I say something about one of his faults you always defend him. I don't notice you defending me so much."

Tony: "How can I defend you? If I defend you to Dad he gets mad. So I can't win no matter what I do!"

Mother: "Well, we're both doing the best we can, and that's how it is!"

Now let's see how the same scene would go with Mother using the feedback technique in which she merely tries to feed back Tony's feelings and not give her own point of view at all. Here's how it would work:

Tony: "I just hate the way you and Dad are always quarreling, Mom. It just makes me sick!"

Mother: "It really makes you feel terrible the way Dad and I are always quarreling."

Tony: "Yes, and you're always saying bad things about him. He is my dad, you know."

Mother: "You don't like it when I say bad things about him because he's the only dad you have."

Tony: "Yeah, and if I say something nice about him you get mad, and if I say something nice about you to him he gets mad. So I can't win no matter what I do!"

Mother: "So you feel like you're between a rock and a hard place, Tony. If you say something nice about him to me, you're afraid I'm gonna get angry. And if you say something nice about me to him, you're afraid he's gonna get angry. So you just don't know what to do!"

Tony: "That's right, I just don't know what to do!"

Notice that when mother uses the feedback technique she does not argue with any of Tony's feelings. She doesn't try to win him over with rational arguments. She does one thing and only one thing: She feeds back in her own words the feelings he is telling her. She does not try to talk him out of any of his feelings: rejection, anger, fear, whatever. She is merely an ally who is listening and understanding his feelings.

You can't prevent your child from having negative feelings —your child isn't going to get rid of his negative feelings in several weeks or a month. And there's no sense in your trying to pull the negative feelings out of him. Instead, give him a chance to vent his feelings in his own time, and show him you understand by reflecting the feelings back to him.

If you would like more details on how to use the feedback technique, consult the chapter "The Feedback Technique" in my book *How to Discipline with Love* and Dr. Thomas Gordon's book *Parent Effectiveness Training*.

There are several factors that determine how well a child gets through the divorce process psychologically. The first is his ability to handle stress. A child's stress-handling ability is determined mostly by his self-esteem and self-confidence. At one extreme is the child who is thrown for a terrible loss, psychologically almost wiped out, by the hostility of his parents to each other and the divorce itself. He has few psychological resources within himself and is almost completely dependent on his parents for his happiness and psychological esteem. When his parents, due to their own misery and difficulties, are unable to provide this for him, he folds under.

At the other extreme is the child with strong self-esteem who is not that dependent on his parents for his internal well-being. He will be unhappy at his parents' stress and at the divorce, but since he has plenty of inner strength, he can ride out the troubles of his parents.

The ability of the child to handle and express his own angry feelings is also crucial to how he weathers the divorce. The child who is unable to handle his angry feelings and buries them inside instead of expressing them has the type of personality that will be affected severely by the divorce. But the child who can handle and express his angry feelings will get them out of his system. He will not let them fester inside.

Another factor that determines how a child will survive the divorce process is, as I mentioned before, the way in which the parents relate to each other during this painful time. When parents do not burden the child with portions of the hostility they feel toward the spouse, they give the child a priceless gift: the gift of not being drawn into the chaotic maelstrom of his parents' anger. The child knows that his parents are very angry at each other, but it doesn't spill over onto him. It is an enormous help to a child during the divorce process if he knows for sure that his parents are angry at each other but not at him.

You can see from this discussion that it is foolish to try to talk about a "typical child of divorce." There is no such thing. Every child is different and will survive the divorce differently, depending on internal and external factors in his life. The same is true for a bereaved child: He will weather the storm as well as his internal and external worlds will allow.

Just remember that if you handle your child well during this time, his losses need not leave him psychologically impaired. Be sure to give him a chance to ventilate his feelings of suffering. Say to him things like, "I know you feel just terrible that your daddy died, and I know you miss him a whole lot. I miss him too. But I love you very much, and you are a wonderful little boy. We both feel very sad right now, but after a while we will begin to feel better."

Or say to him things like, "I know you feel just terrible that Daddy and I are going to get a divorce and not live together anymore. But Daddy will come to see you a lot and he will still love you as he does now. Daddy and I are getting a divorce from each other, but we are not getting a divorce from you. We never will." Then let him tell you his unhappy feelings.

The grieving period for a child of divorce or bereavement will last perhaps six months or a year. But if you feel after some time that your child is still overwhelmed psychologically by the death of his family and that this is more than you can handle, take him to a professional for help.

7. Parenting Children Alone

The child-raising skills required by a single parent are essentially the same as those required by parents in an intact family. If you are not familiar with the ins and out of basic parenting techniques, then I suggest you read my earlier books: *Your Child, How to Parent,* and *How to Discipline with Love.* In them you will find what you need to know to do a bang-up job of raising children. I will not repeat in this book the skills I have delineated in those other books. Instead, I will emphasize the unique ways you need to use those skills, which are different from the ways you would use them if you were the parent in an intact family.

I think the first and most important thing you need to do as a single parent, in relation to your children, is to establish *who has the power in the family.* In theory, of course, you do. But in over twenty years as a psychologist I have encountered many families (both single-parent and two-parent) in which the children rather than the parents have the power. And when the children have the power, then the game of parenting is lost before it begins.

We often learn best by extremes, so I want to give you an extreme example of child power/parent helplessness. This incident was told to me by a patient of mine in his early forties. He had been on several dates with this thirty-five-year-old woman, and for their next date he had invited her to go camping with him over the weekend. She accepted. She told him that her high school senior daughter was going to drive her to his house and have the use of the car the rest of the weekend. But when the mother and the girl arrived, the mother beckoned him off to the side. She said, "Becky has been beating on me all the way down and telling me I'm crazy to go camping with a man I've only known for a few weeks.

She's really mad at me. And when she gets mad she can stay mad a long time! So I think I'd better not go."

My patient was absolutely thunderstruck. "This is incredible, Roberta. You are the teenager and she is the parent! You're allowing her to tell you what you can and cannot do. Do you realize what this is going to do to your daughter when she gets married? She'll be so used to bossing you, she'll assume she's going to do the same thing with her husband, until she runs into a buzz saw."

"Well, I'm sorry, Steve, I just can't go camping with you. But we can arrange some other kind of date that Becky can't find anything wrong with."

"Oh, no, we can't. As a prospect for a real relationship, I wouldn't touch you with a ten-foot pole. This is the most incredible thing I've ever run into, and I don't intend to run into it again. When you start running your family instead of letting Becky run it, give me a ring."

Instead of being like Roberta, who is clearly under Becky's thumb, here is a positive model for you to imitate.

Do you remember back in junior high and high school when you had a substitute for the regular teacher? Usually the class ganged up on the substitute and made his or her life miserable. Let's face it, few substitutes knew how to keep control of a class. But there was one exception to this. I encountered him when I was in my sophomore year in high school. His name was Mr. Dennaburg—Jerry Dennaburg. He was our substitute gym teacher, and I remember to this day how he took charge of our class.

He stood up straight and tall and was utterly silent at first. When he had our attention he began to talk softly. But he could be easily heard throughout the class.

"I'm Mr. Dennaburg, and we have only two rules in this class! If both you and I cooperate and do what we're supposed to, we'll get along fine. But if somebody decides to act up and be a smartass, then he's in trouble. OK?"

He proceeded to give some more instructions on how the different aspects of the class—volleyball, basketball, etc.— would be run.

After he had been talking for about five minutes, a voice from the back row said, "Dennaburg's a jerk!"

Mr. Dennaburg immediately spotted where the voice came from.

"You!"

"Yes, sir."

"What's your name?"

"Wilkins."

Mr. Dennaburg pulled a little tablet from his pocket, scribbled on it, and tore the page off.

"Take this and go to the principal's office. And I wouldn't stop anywhere on the way, because I expect to have a prompt conference with the principal about you."

"Yes, sir."

At that first meeting with Mr. Dennaburg, all of us knew that he was no ordinary substitute teacher. He didn't yell at us like Mr. Huston: "OK, YOU KIDS—don't think you're gonna put anything over on me, cuz you're not!" And he didn't try to buddy up to us like Mr. Sneedly: "Now, we can have a wonderful time together in this class if we'll all work together for the common good. That certainly makes sense, doesn't it?"

We could tell with those two teachers that they were not really sure they had the power of the class. They showed that in their manner. But Mr. Dennaburg showed from the beginning that he had the power and he knew it.

That, in essence, is what you will try to be like as the new single mother of the family. First, you need to call a meeting of the family (at a time which will not be interrupted by anything—a favorite TV program, a meal, homework). The basic purpose of the meeting is to establish who has the power, although you don't state this in so many words. If your children are preschoolers, of course, it will be easier than if they are teenagers. And if your children are already accustomed to well-established parental power, it will be easier than if the children are accustomed to defying parental power whenever they want to.

But in any case, the mother as the new president of the family is a new situation, and you have to start out with new ground rules. Here is the message you need to give your children. Put it into your own words and deliver it in your own way. If you are delivering it to children whose father has died, you will want to soften the tone. But all children feel better knowing that their parent is in charge of things. This is true for children of divorce as well as bereaved children, even if they don't act like they like it.

As I said, put this message in your own words:

"OK, guys, now all of you will get your chance to talk at this meeting. And no one is allowed to criticize what anybody else says. I'm going to talk first because I'm the parent.

"Everything is different now because we're a single-parent family instead of a double-parent family. Daddy isn't here." (Then add a few words about how their divorced father still loves them and will still see them, but he's no longer a member of the family. Or a few words about how much you all miss their dead father, what his role was in the family, and how part of it will now be taken over by you.)

"So now I'm in charge of the family, and we need to have new rules.

"First of all, there's less money to go around, and that means there's less money for me to spend and less money for you kids to spend. I'm sorry about that, but that's the way it is, and you might as well know it from the beginning.

"Second, we will all have to pitch in and help to get the chores around the house done. I've got a list of the things that need doing regularly. Rather than my arbitrarily picking out the things for each of you, I want first to give you a chance to pick what you would rather do." (You display a chart of the different household chores in large print and have the kids choose. The ones that nobody chooses you assign to them, amid huge squeals of protest. Be sure to put yourself down for several chores, such as cooking.) Once all the chores are assigned, ask if anyone has anything to say. They will!! Allow them to speak their feelings, including any type of resentment. But enforce the two rules of only one person talking at a time and nobody criticizing what somebody else says.

When they are all finished, say something like this: "Now, we all know what chores we need to do. If we all do our part and pull together, we're going to have a terrific family—so let's do it!" Then finish off the meeting with some kind of eats all the kids like or a visit to the ice cream store.

What if someone says, "Suppose somebody doesn't do her

chores?" A good answer is, "The penalty for that is sudden death."

On the other hand, once your plan is put into effect suppose one of the kids does not do her chores. How do you handle this? Go on a cooking strike for a day: Cook for the other kids but not the chore avoider. If she keeps on avoiding her chores, you keep on not cooking her meals. As soon as she starts doing her chores, then you start cooking for her again. Or go on a strike where you don't wash or iron their clothes. Or go to the movies.

I'm well aware that it is not easy for you to call such a meeting and chair it. I'm not asking you to feel good and at ease about it. I'm just asking you to do it. Because unless you call such a meeting and establish your authority as parent early, you are going to be in big trouble later.

The children are much easier to work with in the early stages of their separation shock, whether or not they are showing how upset they are. And they will respond much more favorably to the voice of a firm leader then, than they will a few months or a year later.

If you think handling a meeting like this (and following through on it) is more than you can do, then buy a few visits to a professional counselor to help you get the self-confidence to do it. Pulling yourself up by your bootstraps and taking charge of the family may not be easy during your own separation shock, but that is when it needs to be done.

You should have a meeting with the children once a week on a weeknight, not a weekend. Give everybody a chance to talk and air whatever gripes they may have. Do not prolong the meeting too long. Call it the Family Meeting. Always close it with some good eats or something else the children all enjoy.

After you have established who is boss, the next thing to do is set up a positive reward system for your kids. This will help instill a spirit of cooperation in them so that you do not have to hang over them constantly to see that they are doing what you want. The positive reward system is an enormous boon to a parent. And it will stand your children in good stead in later life because it helps them to become self-motivated.

Tattoo this motto on your knee: *Every action of a child that is rewarded with something positive will grow stronger and be more likely to be repeated.* This means that when your child does something she is supposed to, reward her with a hug, a kiss, a word of praise, perhaps an ice cream cone or a special half hour of time with you. Be alert too for times when your child is simply being good—playing quietly, not throwing things, going to bed without fussing—and reward those frequently with a hug or kiss and an affectionate word. You will find your child's behavior becoming gradually more positive if it has not been this way before.

Very few parents, single or double, use this system. Instead, they threaten. They yell. They spank. They lecture. And many other foolish things which do absolutely nothing to change a child's behavior.

If you keep your eye out for any *good* behavior of your children and reward them for it, you will be strengthening all kinds of good behavior. You will also find that the positive reward system makes for a more cheerful household. If you're not sure exactly how to set up a positive reward system for your children, consult the chapter on the positive reward system in my book *How to Discipline with Love.*

Above all, do not believe the myth of the broken home—the myth that says every child of a broken home is bound to turn out psychologically maladjusted. It is simply not true, and you are proving that. For you are already on the road to raising your children to be happy and productive adults.

Another important thing to do as a single parent is to create order and structure in your newly single-parent family. If you already have a job, continue at your work. If you don't have a job, get one. The fact that you have to get up in the morning and turn out certain work in connection with your job is psychologically good for you. Even if you are so well fixed financially that you don't need to work, I still suggest you get at least a part-time job. This will force you to involve yourself in the world of adults and prevent you from hiding away in the tight little circle of your family.

You may think of your children as a tremendous burden which you are forced to carry on top of all of your feelings of loss. In one sense they are undeniably a burden to you. But in another sense, you can thank God for the burden. For their demands on you, like the demands of a job, will force you to keep going. Coping with your children and their problems will take your mind off your own problems. Both a job and your children actually help create the structure your life needs at this time.

As a single parent you should now consider your children's need for a father surrogate. Both a boy and a girl need a father surrogate. A boy needs a man to identify with and model himself after. A girl needs a model for the man she will ultimately marry. Without their father, your children are missing something important. Perhaps you can find a relative or in-law who can play an active male role with your children. A man you are dating should not try to do this unless you and he have settled down to a steady relationship. And I recommend that you not bring the men you are dating into your children's lives very much until you feel ready to settle down to a steady relationship with one of them. One of the best things you can do is hire a high school or college boy to take your children places and do things with them. All in all, I think this is the best thing.

Another important thing you can do for yourself is to stay physically fit. Activity keeps the juices flowing and chases the blues. If you are middle-aged or over, regular exercise is especially important. In his book *Vigor Required,* Dr. Herbert DeVires reports on a research study which found that exercise can positively rejuvenate older people. His study showed that his three-hours-a-week program of controlled exercise helped men and women in their seventies to regain much of the vigor and physical function of their forties.

As a single parent you may have to contend with all sorts of advice on everything you do: sell the house, buy a house, rent a house, rent an apartment, be more relaxed with the kids, get tougher with the kids, start dating, don't date anyone for six months, get a job, quit your job, and on and on. This advice will come from friends, parents, in-laws, and neighbors. It is all free and it will be worth exactly what it costs—nothing.

You will no doubt feel angry and guilty at this time and be in general turmoil. You probably have feelings of fear about whether you can handle 100 percent of the responsibility of raising a family by yourself. (Especially if your husband is not there to keep contact with the kids.) You feel helpless and dependent sometimes, like a little girl suddenly put in charge of a large corporation and expected to run it. While acknowledging these feelings, don't grasp at the free advice offered. Ignore it. Try to set new, flexible goals.

First, ask yourself, *what kind of job do I want, and am I qualified for it?* If you already have a job outside the home, ask yourself, "Is this the job I want?" If you have had no job previously, then you probably need to find one or train for it. Many colleges have counselors who will help you make these decisions. If you suddenly have your husband's estate to handle, this may keep you very busy for a while.

Second, *what separate goals do I have for each of my children?* This means both short-term and long-term goals.

Third, *what new goals do I have for my personal life?* Ask yourself what activities really interest you and what ones you'd like to become interested in. Consider what kind of social life you'd like—who are the friends you'd really like to remain in contact with. Ask yourself what qualities you are looking for in a man. Here are one woman's answers to that, not necessarily in order of importance: (1) intelligence, (2) sense of humor, (3) being a really nice and kind person, (4) a good communicator of both positive and negative feelings, (5) a person who turns me on sexually, and (6) a good bed partner. And if you find a man who has these qualities, hold onto him!

8. A Day in the Life of a Single Parent

Several years ago, a patient of mine described the plight of a single parent very well. She said, "Dr. Dodson, being a single parent is like being a juggler. After six months of practice, you have finally been able to juggle four balls at once. But just as soon as you are able to do that, somebody throws a new ball to you! That's being a single parent," she said.

Here is a typical day in the life of a single parent. The cat has climbed a tree in the yard. Your fourteen-year-old has been caught smoking pot in the boys' room at school. Your nine-year-old has left his lunch at home. Your sixteen-year-old cannot find the encyclopedia and she has a paper due tomorrow.

How does a single mother handle these crises? Let's see an unfortunately all-too-typical single mother in action.

The telephone rings in the XYZ business office. Another office worker answers the phone.

"Muriel, it's for you."

"Who is it?"

"It's your son Jason."

"Ask him what he wants."

"He says he's lost his lunch."

"He lost his lunch?! Tell him I'm right in the middle of typing an important report. I'll call back in ten or fifteen minutes."

"He says he has to talk to you *now.*"

"Tell him I'll call him in fifteen minutes and hang up the phone."

Five minutes later Jason calls back.

"I lost my lunch."

"Listen, Jason, if you took care of your things and knew where they were, you wouldn't be having these troubles."

"You're mean, Mom! You always talk mean to me!!"

"I'm not mean. I'm just telling you what's true. Now, where did you put your lunch?"

"I don't know!"

"All right. If you don't know where you put your lunch, we'll just have to get you another one. Go down to the cafeteria and buy your lunch."

"Mom, I don't have any money."

"Jason, go to the office and borrow money from somebody there."

"I'm scared to do that. I don't know anybody in the office."

"Jason, you know Mrs. Christopher. Borrow the money from her."

"I'm scared to!"

"Jason! If you don't get down there right now and borrow the money from Mrs. Christopher, I'm going to give you something to be scared of! Jason, stop sniveling and do what I tell you!"

"OK! OK! OK!"

Notice what happens in this mother/child interaction. First of all, the child is made to wait to talk to his mother longer than he can comfortably handle. Then when he does get to talk to her, she does not let him know she understands how he feels. Though he starts out with the problem of losing his lunch, his mother gives him an extra problem on top of that. She attacks him verbally, which undermines his feeling of self-esteem. She does not in any way show she truly understands what he is going through.

So let's see how she could have handled this situation in a better way. The phone rings in the office.

"It's for you, Mrs. Single. It's your son Jason."

"Jason, I can't talk long now because I have an important job to do for the next half hour. What's wrong?"

"I lost my lunch."

"And you've looked for it but can't find it anywhere?"

"Yes."

"OK, then, I guess you'll have to buy a lunch today."

"I don't have any money, Mom."

"Well, you can borrow some from Mrs. Christopher in the office."

"I don't like to borrow money in the office."

"Well, I guess you have a choice of borrowing money and eating lunch that way or not eating lunch."

"OK, Mom."

"OK, Jason. Sorry you lost your lunch and I'll see you when I get home tonight."

Notice that this time Mrs. Single did not attack Jason and she spent her time in pointing out what options he had in getting a substitute lunch. She showed him how to solve the problem of getting a lunch and did not add an extra problem for him by attacking him. Most of the problems we will be talking about in this chapter will involve problems at school or home which disrupt, or potentially disrupt, the work of the single mother at the office.

Let me tell you a true incident which forms a very good role model of how to handle something like this. One time when Robert Kennedy was attorney general of the United States, he was having an important press conference at the White House. Approximately seventy media people were in attendance. Suddenly Kennedy's six-year-old son came in the room and went up to his father and whispered something to him. Kennedy held up his hands and spoke to the group of people. "I'm sorry, ladies and gentlemen, but I need to speak to my son for a few minutes." He took him off in the corner and they talked. In about ten minutes Kennedy solved the problem that was bothering his son. His son walked out of the room and Kennedy resumed his press conference.

I think that was a beautiful way to handle the situation. Kennedy did not require his son to wait until the conference was over, for he knew that was too long for a six-year-old to wait. He turned immediately to his son and got the problem solved. Then he was able to go back to give his complete attention to the press conference. If he had told his son he would be with him as soon as the press conference was over, the son probably would have been disrupting the press conference by continually trying to talk to his father.

So whenever your child wants your immediate attention about something which is bothering him, give it to him then.

If you try to put him off, you will certainly lose much more time than if you talk to him right away.

One important way to handle crises is to decide ahead of time what you are going to do in certain situations. And tell your children ahead of time what the policy will be in time of crisis. Now, of course, you will not be able to figure out ahead of time everything that could go wrong. But you can establish policy.

For example, if the child leaves something at home, whether a book for class or something promised to a friend, the policy will be that he can bring it to school the next day. But nobody is going to make a special trip to school to bring it because Mother cannot take time off from work to bring something to school. If a child leaves a schoolbook at home, he can bring it to school the next day. If he forgets lunch, he will buy lunch. He will always have money in his pocket for emergencies. Your child may not like this policy, but he will know ahead of time what the policy is. And he will not expect you to be a chauffeur for the various objects he has left at home.

The problem may involve the home rather than the school.

If the crisis involves fire breaking out in the home, I think it is important not merely to tell your children verbally what to do, but to role play them as you do it. After all, that's why schools have fire drills.

More than simply telling the children what to do verbally, a fire drill helps it to sink into their minds and memories much more deeply. So guide your children in a fire drill of what they should do if a fire breaks out in different parts of the house. Be sure you have fire drills for what to do if the fire occurs when the children are asleep.

I know of a situation where the mother was out for the weekend and the father and three children were at home. A fire was started by faulty wiring in the TV set. The fire broke out in the middle of the night when the father and children were asleep. The father rescued one youngster but the fire spread so swiftly he was not able to rescue the other two in an upstairs room. He was simply unable to get to them in time. And he suffered major burns all over his body trying to rescue them. If the children had practiced what to do in such a situation, they might have been able to rescue themselves. And don't let anybody poke fun at you and say you're going to too much trouble about this. Fire should never be underestimated. You are only taking reasonable precautions in using your fire drills.

The problem may be an intruder wanting to get in the house. The answer to this is to teach your children not to let an intruder in. Teach them under no circumstances to let a stranger in the house. If a stranger needs to make a phone call or has any other reason to ask to be let in, tell him to go to the next house.

This is such an important point, I think it would be wise not merely to tell your children this but to role play it also. Because role playing will fix it in their minds much more powerfully than merely stating the point.

Gather your kids around and say something like this to them:

"OK, kids, now I want you to playact something so that you'll know how to handle it if the situation comes up. I'll pretend I'm ringing the front door bell and only one of you is at home to answer it. OK, here's the bell ringing. *Briiinnng!*"

"Little boy, my husband is terribly sick in the car outside and I need to get him to a doctor as fast as I can. Can I use your phone just for a minute?"

"No, I can't let you do that."

"What do you mean you can't let me do that? I'm telling you my husband is sick and I need to phone the doctor."

"I can't let you in to phone the doctor."

"What's the matter with you? Didn't your mother teach you any manners? I've got to do something for my sick husband and I need to use your phone."

"But I can't let you do that."

"Maybe my husband will die and it'll be your fault. Now let me in!"

"No, I can't do that."

"Well, what am I going to do then?"

"Use the phone next door."

"I'm going to phone your mother later this afternoon and tell her how mean you were to not let me use your phone!"

"Go ahead."

"All right. You'll be sorry you didn't let me use your phone. Good-bye!"

This time the stranger tries using a bribe.

"Little boy, I've got a little boy just like you out in my car and he's very sick. I need to phone the doctor for him. Can I use your phone?"

"No, I'm sorry. You can't."

"What do you mean I can't? This is an emergency and my little boy might die. All you need to do is let me use your phone. It'll only take a minute!"

"I'm sorry. I can't let you."

"All right. Look! Do you like candy bars?"

"Sure!"

"Well, here's two nice big candy bars. You can have them if you open the door."

"No, I'm sorry. I can't do that."

"Don't you want the candy bars?"

"Sure, but I can't open the door for you."

"All right. You'll be sorry!"

Use the role playing with each youngster in your family until you feel sure they know how to resist the bribes or blandishments any stranger might offer.

If the stranger persists, then teach your youngster to dial 911 to get rid of them.

"Now listen, little boy! You're not being a bit of help to me. I need to use your phone and you're being mean not to let me!"

"Ma'am, if you don't go away right now, I'm going to call 911 and tell them to make you stop bothering me!"

"All right, I'm going, but you'll be sorry you didn't help me!"

If one of your children is hurt or injured, this constitutes a different type of emergency. In this situation they should phone you and let you know that someone is hurt or injured and tell you what is wrong. Then if the injury is serious, you can immediately phone your doctor and head for home. If for any reason your child can't get you at the office, he should phone your doctor himself. Have the doctor's office number in large numerals posted by the telephone. If the situation does not seem to be serious to you, you may go home and take care of it or phone a neighbor to help take care of it.

From your adult point of view, it will seem to you that at various times your child will be phoning you at the office about ridiculous things that he should be able to take care of himself. And you will be tempted to tell him that what he's calling about is ridiculous. But what seems ridiculous in your eyes may not be ridiculous in his eyes. So remember that he would not call you at all if he were not upset about something. You may feel, "Well, if he's lost his lunch, then he can simply buy a new one and the problem is solved." Well, if he could see it that way he would do it. So obviously he wants some kind of reassuring word from you about how to solve the problem. If he could solve the problem by himself, he wouldn't need to phone you.

This is why it's important for you to use the feedback technique (pages 40–41) whenever possible when responding to your child's anxious phone calls. For example, your sixth grader, Sandy, phones you from school. She's crying.

"Mom, something terrible has happened!"

"What is it, Sandy?"

"I lost my yearbook."

"Well, don't worry. We'll look at the lost and found in school and see if they found it. And if worse comes to worst, you can always buy a new one."

"No, I can't, Mother! Because this had the autographs of everybody in my class. I can't replace it. It's just gone and I'll never get it back!" (She cries.)

At this point do not say, "Now, don't worry, Sandy. I'm sure you'll get it back." Instead, reflect her feelings something like this:

"That really makes you feel terrible because you're afraid you'll never get it back. And it had all the autographs of the other people in the class."

A response such as this recognizes the reality of your child's feelings and shows you understand how awful she feels. So don't just respond to your child on a purely rational level. Respond on the level of her feelings.

The basic problem that I have been sketching out in these situations is that you have a full-time job to handle. If you do not handle phone calls from your children in a wise manner, you may find that they are beginning to pile up on you at work. Of course, no single mother can know ahead of time exactly what kinds of emergency phone calls she will get at work.

Here is another way to handle this situation. Find a capable college or high school student and let him or her become your ombudsman. You may not be familiar with this term. An ombudsman is someone in a government position who is supposed to handle any type of problem which may come up. So you can select an ombudsman and introduce him or her to your children. Tell them that Mike, the ombudsman, will handle any minor problems that come up, minor problems that are not important enough to phone you about. Actually, I think it wise to have two ombudsmen so that either one of them is available during your work hours.

One final suggestion on how to handle the potentially vexing problem of phone calls. Whenever a problem comes up that is difficult to handle for which your youngster contacts you at work, role play this situation when you get home that day. One thing that is particularly difficult to handle by telephone is conflict between children.

"Mommy, Linda is watching TV all the time and won't let me see what I want!"

"You're a liar! Mommy, she's not telling the truth! She didn't even want to watch TV until I turned it on!"

"You're the liar! LIAR! LIAR!"

"You call me a liar again and I'm going to hit you!"

"Mommy! She hit me!"

"All right, you two, now listen carefully. I want you to call Mike, the ombudsman. You've got his phone number right there by the telephone. And Mike is going to help you two settle the problem of the television. You can talk it over with him and whatever he decides is final."

You will find it very helpful to spend a little time educating your ombudsman with two important techniques for handling children. One is the feedback technique and the other is the mutual problem-solving technique. You can find a chapter on each of these in my book *How to Discipline with Love*.

Talk over the points of these two chapters with your ombudsman and make sure he understands them. Role play the techniques with him. This way, when you have conflicts about anything in the family, the ombudsman should be skillful in handling them.

Generally, problems of conflict between the children are quite difficult to handle over the phone. They need somebody there on the immediate scene. But you can't keep hopping back and forth from the office to the home. That's where the ombudsman can take your place and get the children together and playing decently again.

My impression is that many single parents have no overall strategy for handling crisis phone calls from either home or school. This is what I have tried to present to you in this chapter. The strategy is geared to enabling you to spend the least amount of time being interrupted at your daily work. And to enable your children to feel you are there when they need help but to keep their requests to you at a minimum.

We also need to discuss in this chapter the various situations that call for some cooperation on the part of the divorced parents. For example: how to handle graduation? If the divorced parents are reasonably neutral with one another there is no reason they cannot sit together with the child. But if the parents are full of hostility toward one another, they should avoid sitting together. For if they sit together, the child will surely pick up the hostile vibes between the parents and this will probably spoil the graduation.

The same logic holds true for parent-teacher conferences. If the mother and father are reasonably neutral toward one another, then they can attend together. If they are full of hostility, they should attend separately.

If there is a need to discuss a child's school work and the mother and father can be reasonable with one another, then they can discuss it together with the child. If they cannot be reasonable, then it is a total waste of time.

If there are situations where a father is needed but the child's father is out of the picture or temporarily not available, the mother should substitute. For example, a father is ordinarily necessary for a child's membership in Indian Guides or Indian Princesses. But if there is no father available, the mother can substitute.

What should the mother or father do if one of them thinks the other's way of handling the child is wrong when the child is with the other parent? Answer: Zip your lip! When the child is with you, then you determine the best way to handle him. When the child is with the other parent, that parent determines the best way and neither of you should attempt to tell the other how to raise the child.

When a parent remarries, should the child attend the wedding? Certainly. Unless he doesn't want to. Your stand should be neutral. You don't try to talk the child out of it if he wants to attend and you don't try to talk him into it if he doesn't.

9. Custody and Visitation

There is no doubt whatsoever in my mind that joint custody is the best arrangement for both the children and the parents. I vividly recall being a psychologist expert witness and one among others who helped to create the first joint custody situation in the state of Colorado. The two children, aged six and eight, were to stay four days a week with their mother and three days a week with their father. It was not easy to get everyone to agree to this, but once they did it worked out very well. The children liked it because they got to see a great deal of *both* Mother and Daddy. The parents liked it because they had regular time each week with the children and regular time each week for themselves.

Joint custody will work only when the two parents live close enough so that the child's school will not be disrupted. But the real catch to joint custody is that it will work only with reasonably mature parents. It will not work with immature, hostile, backbiting parents who spend their half week with the children disparaging the other parent.

By joint custody I mean genuine joint physical custody, with the children staying part of a week or a month or six months with each parent in turn (with the other parent having visitation if it's a long period). I do not mean something that is joint custody in name only, where the children actually live exclusively with one parent. That defeats the whole meaning of true joint physical custody.

The court usually gives custody to the mother and visitation to the father. This is not a very good psychological situation for the children, because they get to see relatively little of their father. If I were the mother in such a custody situation, I would try to enlarge the visitation rights of the father. I would do this for two reasons: First, it is good for the children psychologically to see as much of their father as possible. And second, it would give me some relief from the constant presence and emotional demands of the children. If their father were receptive to the idea, I would give him an extra weeknight for dinner or perhaps overnight if he lived close, or an extra weekend on either a regular or irregular basis. In the next chapter I'll give some more guidelines for visitation for fathers without custody.

Unfortunately, many divorced fathers do not want to see their children this often. They weren't terribly interested in the children when they were married, and they are even less interested now. One study of married fathers in intact families with one-year-old children discovered that the fathers spent an average time per day with the child on a one-to-one basis of thirty-seven seconds. Thirty-seven seconds!

What can you do if you've got a thirty-seven-second father on your hands? I'm afraid there's not much you can do. If he doesn't want to see the children often or at all, you can't force him to.

If the children ask why Daddy doesn't come to see them more, turn the question over to them. Say, "I don't know why he doesn't see you more often. Why don't you ask him? And tell him you want to see him more."

Don't ever give phony reasons why Daddy doesn't come see them. That compounds the crime. Then you not only have a father who doesn't visit his children but a mother who lies about it. Don't put yourself in that position. You don't have to bad-mouth your ex-husband, but you don't have to cover up for him by lying about the situation. Just play it low-key. Answer any question your children ask you with the truth.

Whether your custody is joint or single, you should avoid what I call "phony scenes of the happy family." By this I mean where the children, the mother, and the father all get together for Thanksgiving, Christmas, and Easter just as if they were the family they used to be. This is as phony as a three-dollar bill and everyone knows it. They are all very aware that the family is no longer intact. The children will be as tense as tightly strung wires in such an artificial situation.

Sure, Father can celebrate Thanksgiving, Christmas, and Fourth of July with the kids—but at his own place and without you there. By the way, arrangements of this kind can be made between the two of you without spending money on lawyers' fees.

We've spoken of the father who visits the children but visits very little. But what about the father who abandons the children? He may disappear right after the divorce, or he may visit them for a while and then disappear. Or he may continue to live nearby but simply stop seeing them.

All of this may be tied in with a refusal to pay child support, or it may not. We know that after the first year of divorce approximately 80 percent of divorced fathers stop paying child support, which I think is a national scandal. Someday we will have an efficient national system of catching up with fathers who skip out on child support. But unfortunately we don't have such a system now. If a father moves out of state, it's very difficult to catch up with him.

The father who acts this way has actually abandoned his children. And as I advised earlier, the best way to handle your children's questions about it is to say something like, "I don't know why your father doesn't come to see you. I think he's crazy not to come see such wonderful kids like you!"

Sometimes telling the truth about why their father doesn't come to visit, and telling them that he doesn't pay the child support money, is an example of the difference between telling the truth and bad-mouthing. You need to tell the kids why Father doesn't come to visit because they ask you and they want to know. But they probably don't even know there is such a thing as child support and they won't know he's not paying it unless you tell them. On the other hand, if you're in a precarious financial situation and dependent on the child support to keep the family afloat, then you may have to explain why there's no cash for things the children really need. Even then, it's better to be low-key in explaining such things rather than malevolent. The children must adjust to the facts, but a lot of heat and anger from you will only make the adjustment tougher.

Now, what about the father who has moved a long distance away because of his job situation but still comes to see the children and pays child support faithfully? You can help foster a strong long-distance relationship between the children and their father in many ways. For example, you might buy a small tape recorder and help them make tapes to send their father. Or help them make up a little newspaper (hand printed or with cut-out words and pictures) with news of each of the children in it.

If you leave their father's birthday up to the children, they'll probably forget it. Then he'll be hurt and that will be a rupture in their relationship, which isn't good for anybody. So remind the children of their father's birthday and Father's Day and Christmas, and help them to choose and send cards and presents.

Above all, remember: What's good for the relationship between the children and their father is good for the children. And what's good for the children is good for you!

No matter how far away the children's father lives, we do have airplanes in this country now. And if you and their father can arrange a one- or two-week (or even more) trip to visit him in the summer after school is out, that will be a wonderful thing for everybody. Father and the kids will get to see each other in person for a week or so, and you will get a vacation from being a parent. And that will do all of you good!

Now, we come to the most unpleasant situation of all: the father who hassles his ex-wife. Many a mother has gritted her teeth and finally made it through the divorce, then settled back and thought to herself, *Well, it was awful, but thank God it's all over.* The next day an officer of the court arrives at the front door bearing a subpoena. And she realizes it's not all over.

Under our legal system anybody can sue anybody they want to about anything. And your ex-husband can sue you about anything he wants as long as his money holds out for lawyers' fees. You will need to get a lawyer to defend yourself, and that costs you money. I wish I had some magic answer to this terrible problem, but I don't. I can only say this: Don't attempt to act as your own lawyer. You have had no legal training, and the opposing lawyer will probably make mincemeat of you. If you don't have enough money for a lawyer, ask the court to appoint you one. Or ask the court to have the father pay your lawyer's fees.

I know divorced couples who have sued and countersued each other for six to ten years after the divorce was granted

—an incredible emotional mess for everybody, including the children. But nevertheless they did it.

Unfortunately, there are also fathers who hassle you out of court. In this case, it's sometimes necessary to go through the trouble and expense of issuing legal restraints and injunctions to stop the problems.

I wish there were a simple, quick, easy solution to the problem of the hassling father. If I knew one I would write a book about it, make a million dollars, and retire!

I do have one important word of advice: Never take it lightly when the father takes you to court. You may laugh at the ridiculous charges, but the judge may not, especially if your ex-husband has enough witnesses prepared to say that the charges against you are true. From your divorce experience you may have learned that a great deal of lying goes on in court. If so, be prepared for a lot of lying if your ex-husband takes you to court now. Take every legal battle seriously and get a lawyer—a good lawyer—to defend you.

One final word about visitation: Many times a judge will grant the father "reasonable visitation." This is a very bad ruling from both the mother's and father's point of view because it is vague and indefinite. Nobody knows what "reasonable visitation" is. Can you imagine a judge's granting a mother "reasonable child support?"

Visitation rights should be spelled out as clearly as child support is. We have said it is good for the children to see their father as much as possible. If the court specified that he may have them Tuesdays for dinner, Friday evenings, every other weekend, one week at Christmas, spring vacation, and two weeks in summer, they are going to see each other regularly and often. The children can count on it and look forward to it. This is infinitely better than "reasonable visitation." It guarantees that the children get to see their father even if you should be temporarily mad at him and be tempted to change your mind about when he can have them. So it's better for you, because it's good for the children.

I've already stressed the importance of not speaking ill of your ex-husband to the children. But when they visit him, what if he says negative things about you? There's nothing you can do to keep him from saying whatever he pleases about you. But you can be strong enough to resist the temptation to bad-mouth him in return. Even if you do slip once in a while and say something mean about him, you can apologize to the children for doing it. You can say, "Kids, I was upset and mad when I called your father names the other day. I was wrong to do that. I just lost my temper and said things I shouldn't have." Chances are that their father will not apologize as you just did, so your apology gives your children a lesson in maturity they would not get if you were not their parent.

One thing I know you would not do, no matter how tempted you might be, is to try to prevent or mess up your ex-husband's visitation. Unfortunately, a lot of mothers do exactly that. You can just refuse to resort to such bitter and vindictive tactics. The mother who interferes with visitation is showing her hostility to the father, which is what she means to do. But she is also hurting her children deeply because they love their father and need to see him. So if you need to express hostility to your ex-husband, do it in other ways, not those which hurt your children.

There will always be anger and bitter feelings in a divorce. But hopefully, these will settle down after a while and the two of you, though divorced, will be able to cooperate in raising your children.

10. The Father Without Custody

In the overwhelming number of cases the mother ends up with custody of the children. This is why I am writing this chapter to the father. I also suggest that he go back and read chapter 9, "Custody and Visitation," if he has not already done so.

We can divide noncustodial fathers into two groups. First are those who really don't care much about their children. These range from fathers who see their children only sporadically to fathers who abandon their children completely.

On the other hand, there are fathers who care a lot about their children. If they live nearby, they visit regularly. If they have had to move away because of a job or other reason, they still manage to keep in touch. They make tape recordings for the children. They phone. They send postcards or packages with little gifts. They arrange a week's or two weeks' visit in the summer. In one way or another, they keep alive a deep and loving bond between themselves and their children.

Mothers should be grateful for fathers like this. For the love of the father is an important foundation in building the self-esteem of a child.

Unfortunately, some mothers don't seem to care about this. Some are so filled with hatred toward the father that they do everything they can to keep him from deepening his emotional bonds with his children. Here is merely one example among many I could give:

This was told me by a thirty-eight-year-old father. He and the mother had been divorced for five years, and she had done everything she could to interfere with his child visitation. Her latest commando raid occurred when the oldest boy was eleven, and he and his father were joining the Boy Scouts together. The mother went to see the scoutmaster and told him the father was an immoral influence on the boy. She said that the scoutmaster should not allow the father to go on hikes and outings with the son. Without making any effort to verify these charges, the scoutmaster forbade the father to attend their hikes.

The only thing the incensed and furious father could do was take the mother to court, which he did. The judge granted the following injunction: "Hazel Sorkin, you are hereby enjoined from interfering with the father-and-son relationship of Ralph Sorkin and Patrick Sorkin in this Boy Scout troop or any other Boy Scout troop, or in any other extracurricular activity." From then on, Mrs. Sorkin kept her hands off the Boy Scout troop.

Ralph Sorkin told me that in the six years that his ex-wife was a thorn in his flesh, it took him six lawyers (he had to keep weeding out the bad ones) and $23,000 in lawyers' fees to prevent his wife from messing up his relationship with the children (and not every father has $23,000 to spend in court). But he said it was worth it. For you as a father without custody, it's worth hanging in there to do everything you can to prevent your relationship with your kids from being disturbed. It may be only when your kids are nineteen or twenty that they will realize what kind of a father you really are, as compared with the kind of father their mother pictured to them.

Mothers are often not aware of how important the father is to the child. The best single study of divorce I know, that by Wallerstein and Kelley, makes it abundantly clear how eager and even desperate the children are to see their father during and after the divorce process. So the wise mother will do all she can, for the sake of her child, to make it easy for the child and the father to see each other.

Fathers in intact families are sometimes totally ignorant of how little they really know about their children. It is often the mother who interacts with the child, while the father stands by on the sidelines. I have seen this for many years as a psychologist. I ask the mother and father what problems they think the child has. The father says, "Oh, I think he's just a normal boy who gets a little upset at times." Then I ask the mother and she tells me in detail the different problems the boy has. It's as if the father does not even know his son other than what he looks like on the outside.

Fathers who do not really know their children are in for a

real shock when they first begin to visit them during the divorce process. As one father said to me, "I took my four-year-old boy out to dinner and realized after about ten minutes that I didn't even know how to talk to him!"

Many divorced fathers need to *learn* what to do with their children and how to talk to them. My advice to most fathers is this: Don't assume you know much about your child, because you probably don't. Begin by assuming your child is a strange being from outer space and it will take time for you to get to know him. Then your visitation can become an exciting affair: getting to know your child for the first time!

To the father who thinks of spending time with his child as a chore, I wish he could see the scene at home before he comes to visit—the little five-year-old asking his mother over and over what time it is, opening the front door again and again to see if Daddy's there yet. If this father could realize how eager his young child is to see him, he might start thinking of his visit as an adventure and an opportunity, rather than a chore.

There are many "adventures" a father can share with his preschool child, which will delight the youngster's heart and cost absolutely nothing: a visit to a fire station, a police station (where he can get fingerprinted), a newspaper publishing plant, a welding shop, and many others.

When you are first getting rolling on a routine of visiting your child, make the visits fairly frequent, fairly short, and fairly structured. This is a new situation for both of you, so having something specific to do that does not involve a lot of relating may be easier at first. You might go to the park for a couple of hours, to the zoo, or to a movie with a treat afterward. After you and he become more used to being alone together, you can settle into longer, less structured visits, including weekends and vacations together.

It's important to have a regular schedule of visitations and stick to it. Your child needs to know when he will see you, and he needs to be able to count on you to show up. If you can also have occasional spontaneous extra visits, so much the better.

Give some thought in advance as to how you and your child are going to spend your time together. Otherwise, you may find yourself out of ideas midway through the visit. And don't feel you have to keep your child constantly amused when you are together. It's perfectly natural for him to have some TV time while you read for a while, just as if he were at home with you.

Speaking of your home, you should do your best to make your child feel that your home is his. This means designating a separate room, a special corner of your room, or an area of the living room as his, with his own toys, clothes, and the pictures he's drawn. His things should be waiting in his space when he comes to visit.

And now, three words of caution: First, don't overdo on entertaining your child or on gift giving, either out of guilt or because you're trying to outdo his mother. Both are psychologically bad for your child.

Second, it is probably better not to introduce your child to women you are dating, at least not at first. Your child is adjusting to a new kind of relationship with his daddy, and he does not need a strange woman intruding on the scene.

Finally, during your separation shock after the divorce you may find that the sight of your child is a painful reminder of a very unhappy time in your life. Don't let this prevent you from seeing him. He needs you badly, just as you need to have a relationship with him. Tell yourself that the pain you feel is a necessary part of your grief process. Facing it and living through it will help you. Avoiding it is bad for both you and your child.

The cheerful side to all this is that you really are building a new relationship with your child. And you may find, as many divorced fathers do, that the new relationship is much closer than the old. For in your new circumstances you and your child are actually spending more quality time together than you ever have before. This is wonderful for both of you.

Unfortunately, many fathers have been taught to be successful in business but not in nurturing children. And so it is into business that 99 percent of their energy and effort go.

I think of a past patient of mine, a bright and attractive young woman. When she was sixteen, she saw her father only on Christmas and Easter, when the other three children saw him. She yearned to see more of him, for him to be a real father. She kept hinting for him to take her to lunch some-time, but the message never got through to him.

Finally she invited him to lunch and he accepted. He worked about forty minutes by freeway from where she lived, so she made reservations at a restaurant near his work. Every-thing looked as if it was finally coming up roses for her. Then the morning of the luncheon she got a telephone call saying that some unexpected work had come up and her father couldn't make it after all. The phone call was made by her father's secretary.

That did it for the young woman. She made no further effort to see her father, and years later it was as if they were strangers. Someday I think that father will realize he missed something in his relationship with his daughter. And then he will make awkward moves to try to improve the relationship. But it will be too late. He lost her years ago when he didn't keep that luncheon date with his wistful, eager daughter.

Now, what about your child and your women friends? I've said it's probably better not to introduce her to him at first. There is nothing he needs less than a procession of girl friends going in and out of your life and his. When you do bring a girl friend to meet him for the first time, talk the situation over with her first. She may be a mother herself and know something about children. Or she may have never had children and know extremely little about them. A briefing session is called for in any case, because she needs to be prepared for what will probably happen. The child is going to be jealous of that girl friend, no matter what. And this jealousy will diminish only slowly, as he comes to like the friend and realize that she is not really a threat to him. If the girl friend is prepared for this jealousy, she's certainly going to handle it better than if it takes her by surprise.

Some people say that the girl friend of a divorced man should not attempt to "bribe" the child with a toy. She should wait until the child likes her just for herself. I disagree. If it's a preschool child, there's nothing that will get the relation-ship off to a better start than a small toy that he really likes. If he says suspiciously, "Why did you get me this?" she can answer, "Because I know that all children like toys. And be-cause I know you're a child."

The combination of girl friend and your child can be sticky if you're not careful. You hope that he will regard her as someone nice who is an added bonus when he comes to see you. But he is more likely to think of her as someone who is taking you and your interest and time away from him. As one youngster felt, "He can see *her* all week long . . . why does he have to bring her along on *my* visit?"

When you do have your girl friend and your child together, it's wise to reserve intimacies such as hand holding and kissing for private times. A ten-year-old expressed his feelings very clearly: "They hang all *over* each other—it's really disgusting."

So ease your girl friend and your child together, slowly and gently. If she rushes in effusively with heavy gestures of affection, too much too soon, he will back off quickly!

If this lady is the one you eventually decide to marry, you'd better make sure that she likes your children and they like her. If she dislikes them and doesn't know how to get along with them, or if they dislike her, you are going to have real trouble in your marriage. For it is not you alone who is getting married. You are a package deal, and your wife-to-be is marrying the whole package. This is one of the most common errors of remarriage. The two people act as if their love for each other were all that counted and the children's feelings could be ignored. Well, they can't. The children's feelings—both his children and hers—need to be accepting, or the marriage is not going to work.

I've been writing as if we were dealing only with near-home fathers. What about the long-distance father, who may live 400 or 3,000 miles away? What is this father going to do, cut off by long distances from his kids?

First, he can recognize a psychological fact. If he had two preschool children who lived with their mother in San Diego (a large city south of Los Angeles), and he worked as a lawyer in Los Angeles, they would feel almost as remote and far away as when he is living in New York City. So he has no more problems making himself "real" to the kids when he's 3,000 miles away than if he were 130 miles away.

So what can he do to keep contact with his kids in California when he's in New York?

He can send them all kinds of mail. Colorful postcards take only a minute or two to write. If he receives lots of junk mail, he may not be interested in it but his preschoolers might love it. He can buy a special rubber stamp that says MAIL FROM DADDY and label each piece of mail he sends to them with this distinctive stamp. Children of all ages love to receive mail because they get so little of it. They will be happy to get any kind of mail from Daddy.

Next, he can buy an inexpensive tape recorder and talk to the kids by means of this. They can do the same with their tape recorder, especially if Mother helps them. As a matter of fact, Mother's attitude is crucial. If she pooh-poohs the whole idea it will be hard for the kids to be enthusiastic. But if she acts energized about their "talking to Daddy," this gives the whole enterprise a big boost.

One big advantage of a tape recorder is that the kids can play it over and over again (so does Father). And very soon the prices of videotape cameras and players are going to come down to where almost everyone can buy them. The impact of videotape is even more powerful than that of audiotape. The children can not only hear Daddy, they can see him.

But none of these things make up for face-to-face meetings. I hope it is possible for the children to go visit their father in the summer for a week or two, or for him to visit them. Airlines take special care of young children traveling alone and for youngsters aged six to eleven it should be a big thrill —an airplane trip! If the airplane is too expensive and Father is not too far away, a bus can get the children there. I think psychologically it's better for the children to visit Dad than vice versa. But the cost of living being what it is, you may have to negotiate on these things. If Dad has a business trip near where the kids live, he should be able to arrange to stop and see them.

You can be sure of one thing: All of your contact will be deeply appreciated by your children. They may not say this out loud to you (because that's the way children are), but they feel it deep down. And during all of the years between the time of the divorce and the time they became adults, you are strengthening the emotional bond between you. This will make a great difference when the children are older and your status with them is young-adult-friends/older-adult-friend instead of children/father.

Many children of intact families have terrible relationships with their fathers. As soon as they get their first jobs and become financially independent, they want to have little to do with their fathers. But you will be different. You will be a long-distance, divorced father, with children who are now adults who love you and want to spend time with you because of the contact you've kept with them over the years.

Incidentally, in case it has escaped your attention, if you are a nearby father you can do all of the things the long-distance father can do: postcards, tapes, etc. And it will have the same result: It will strengthen the emotional bond between you.

Here's another special thing you can do for your kids, no matter where you live: On the birthdays of each one, write special letters telling them how much you love them and how much each means to you. Praise them for any special accomplishments. Seal the letters and tell them they're not to open it until they've opened the rest of the presents and are alone.

It's really tough when your ex-wife is working against your relationship with your kids. When she has custody, she has zillions of opportunities to cross you up. Any gift you give or correspondence you send can easily be downgraded by a disparaging mother.

If she has it in for you, one of the things the mother can do is upset the visitation schedule. For example, say you have the coming weekend for visitation. You go to the front door and knock; you're all set for a nice weekend. But the children aren't home. Mother has taken them to visit their grandparents. She "forgot" it was your weekend! So it's twenty-five miles out there to get them and twenty-five miles back. You're furious and the kids are confused and you have to choose between the picnic you've planned and the movie you've promised, because there isn't time for both.

If your wife gets really vicious with her sabotage, your only resort may be to take her to court. And that's expensive. This is one of the reasons I'm so strongly in favor of joint custody, which I mentioned earlier. Joint custody helps prevent these kinds of things. I foresee the day when 90 percent of divorces will be joint custody. There are so many advantages to it. The children get to see a lot of both parents, so they have less feeling of having lost their family. And it tends to reduce the bickering by the ex-spouses, as long as both are acting reasonably mature and not trying to sink the deal.

If you want details of joint custody and how it works, I recommend *Mother's House, Father's House* by Isolante Ricci.

If you have the opportunity to work out joint custody, my advice is to try it. If it doesn't work, you are no worse off than you were before. Be sure that you and your ex-wife both have lawyers who believe in this kind of arrangement. Some lawyers are against it. Just remember that children need consistency of environment to be living well.

I have a few more words of advice if your ex-wife is giving you a really bad time, riding roughshod over the rules, and backbiting. You have already tried to get her to see the benefits (to *her* as well as the children) of letting you have the children at the court-ordered times, of not downgrading your other efforts to keep contact with them, of not trying to turn them against you. But she is so mad at you and at life in general that she is like the old proverb—cutting off her nose to spite her face. At the same time she is probably complaining to her neighbors about the high price of baby-sitters, and complaining that the children are wearing her out.

This woman is going to do whatever she can to get back at you for her unhappiness, and there's not much you can do to stop her. So what *can* you do?

The first level of defense is not to do anything. Don't retaliate; it won't work. She's like a two-year-old in the middle of a tantrum. You cannot get through to her, and everything you say will only stir her up more. By keeping silent you are saying, "No comment." And if you do try to reason with her, she will distort your words and accuse you of saying things you didn't.

If she's been bad-mouthing you to the children, what should you do about it? Nothing. There's nothing you can do to prevent it, and you can hope that your nonresponse will reduce her venom sometime in the future.

But aren't her poisonous words about you to the children detrimental to you? Not necessarily. It depends on how old the children are and how sophisticated they are at seeing through her lies. Also, sooner or later, they will notice how different your attitude is from hers. Of course it goes without saying that you should not bad-mouth your wife any more than she should bad-mouth you.

If you take this ex-wife to court, get yourself a witness who has seen her breaking the court rules and who can vouch for your own good behavior. Take this person along when you go to pick up your children, especially if your ex-wife is likely to be present. While you are in court, don't speak to her unless you have a witness with you.

But let's say that you and your ex-wife do not hassle each other. Neither of you backbites or slings mud. Great! You have already accomplished more than most divorced couples. It means that neither of you is interfering with the other's child raising, so each of you is free to do what you think best for the children.

After a few months of this rare and beautiful situation, when you and your ex-wife have gotten to feeling comfortable in keeping quiet about what the other is doing, the two of you might decide to launch some joint efforts. You might, for example, attempt a joint parent-teacher conference (don't include the child being discussed). If this kind of thing is successful, then you will truly be fulfilling your promise to the children: "We both love you and always will, even though we are getting a divorce from each other." In most divorced families it must appear to the child that Mother loves her more than Daddy, because it's Mother who goes to the parent-teacher conferences and Mother who works on the May Day Carnival and the Thanksgiving play.

To be a father without custody is often not easy. Your visitations with the children can interfere with your other plans. Their mother can try to get at you through them. You can feel out of control in helping the children toward the goals you wish for them. But everything you do toward keeping your relationship with them intact and growing makes you a richer man. These are riches that money can't buy, and you are sharing them with your children.

11. Grandparents: A New Resource for the Single Family

Your child's grandparents will probably be very important to you in your job of single parenting. They may be important in either a positive or a negative way, and much of that will depend on how you handle the situation.

Let's begin on the positive side. If both sets of grandparents are the easy-going, flexible, wonderful people that they are, then you and they should have no trouble finding a very positive way for them to help with the raising of your children. First of all, you may need to have one or more than one grandparent help in the daily care of your child while you are at work. The grandparent will probably care more about your child than a paid caretaker and will love your child. It may also help a great deal financially to use the grandparent as a day-care person rather than to have to pay for one. If you are going to use the grandparent as an adjunct to your single parenting in this or in any other way, you will probably find it very helpful to give a copy of my book *How to Grandparent* to the grandparent and read it yourself. Everything that helps the grandparent do a better job of grandparenting helps your child and helps you.

Please don't think that when I talk about using grandparents as day-care persons I am only talking about grandmothers. There is no reason at all that a grandfather cannot be a part-time or full-time day-care person. Many grandfathers can do just as good a job with children as grandmothers and sometimes better. So be sure to put both grandfathers on a possibility list for your day-care needs.

The grandparents may not ask for any pay from you for their day-care duties. Or they may need to be paid something, though not as much as you would pay a non-family member. Regardless of which of these two options you and they decide on, I strongly suggest that you buy them a present from time to time just to show your gratitude.

Whether you use a grandparent as a full-time day-care person or part-time, you may have occasional disagreements on how to handle the children. I suggest you read Dr. Thomas Gordon's book *Parent Effectiveness Training* to learn how to deal with grandparents in a disagreement. Remember that some of the modern ideas of handling children may be quite new to a grandparent. And you should first give the grandparent the freedom to express his or her own views about the subject before giving your or the book's views.

If you find that you are not going to change the grandparent's view on some particular area, then it's probably wise to give up on that. For example: When my wife and I left our preschool youngster with the grandparents for a weekend, Grandma typically would lie down with the boy to get him to sleep. We asked her not to do this because it made it more difficult for us to get him to sleep when he came back home. Though she finally agreed, she kept "forgetting" not to do it. So after a while we decided we were not going to change her behavior in this respect. This would simply be the price we would have to pay for a free weekend babysitter.

I have mentioned the grandparent as a part-time day-care person, and under this category we need to discuss the grandparent as a babysitter. Here you face a great difference of opinion among grandparents. Some love to babysit; some don't like it a bit. Be sure that the grandparent really enjoys babysitting or don't ask. Because if there's no enjoyment, there will probably be resentment underneath and that doesn't do your child any good. And be sure you have times when the three of you—your child, the grandparent, and you —get together. Because otherwise, in the back of the grandparent's mind, he or she is going to think that you just want a babysitter and nothing more.

I think it's a shame that so many grandparents in our society don't have offspring with children of their own who make use of their talents and abilities. After all, parents can't teach children everything. And grandparents can often teach children things that the parents are not able to do or do not have time to do. For example: I do not fish, I am only a very poor welder, and I have no ability at all to handle mechanical things. So my children have learned all of these things from their grandfather on their mother's side. He has been delighted to teach them to fish, to weld, and to make all sorts of things in his home workshop. One of the results is that my son Rusty, who is now twenty-one, has become the chief person in the family to fix anything of a mechanical nature when there is a problem with it.

I think the chances are very strong that in the grandparents you have untapped resources for your family. They probably bring to the family some assets they did not have when they were raising you: more maturity of judgment, more leisure time, and a more mellowed approach.

There is another positive way in which the grandparents can help you. They can give the children a sense of their roots. Children like to know where they come from. They will ask you to tell them what it was like when you were a child. They like to think of themselves as part of a family line that goes back in time and has solidity and permanence. This is where the grandparents can make a unique contribution to the family. Who can impart a sense of living history better than they? You can help this process along. Tell your children to ask the grandparents about what life was like when they were growing up, what happened to them when they were children. By making their living history available to the children, the grandparents are deepening their relationship with the children and strengthening their roots.

Now let's take a look at the possible negative side of you and the grandparents. If you are a single parent by the death of a spouse, there will probably be no negative after-effects of this in your relationship with them as you raise your children. But if you have become a single parent by divorce, there may unfortunately be some negative after-effects.

For one thing, one or both sets of grandparents may strongly disapprove of the divorce. They may disapprove of it simply because they are against divorce. "There has never been a divorce in our family until you!" Or they may strongly disapprove of the reasons for the divorce. They may feel that your spouse was all wrong in getting the divorce. Or they may feel that the fault was mainly yours. In any case, they are probably not going to feel emotionally neutral about the divorce. And how they feel about it certainly affects their relationship with you and with the children.

Here is one very unfortunate grandparent-parent situation regarding a divorce from my case history files. The divorce was a very messy situation. The father had been having an affair with a woman at work. When the mother finally discovered what was going on after about a year, she furiously told her husband to get out. The husband had no deep interest in the other woman and didn't want the marriage to break up. He came to see me to try to save his marriage and he was finally able to persuade his wife to see me also.

The maternal grandparents were swollen with rage. They told their daughter she was lucky to be getting rid of such a rotten man and she was insane to even think of reconciling with him. The grandfather phoned the husband and said, among other things, "If I were twenty years younger, I would give you the thrashing of your life for what you've done to my daughter."

But after a year of counseling, during which time the couple were living apart, they ended up getting back together. They had to deal with some really hot emotions, hate, guilt, and hurt, but they finally got all of them out in the open and worked through them. In the end, I felt that the couple were on solid footing for the first time in their marriage.

Unfortunately, the grandparents had so alienated the mother and father that the parents put a deep freeze on them by preventing them from seeing the grandchildren. I was finally able to help the parents and grandparents to establish a good relationship again. But this is the kind of situation that can work an incredible hardship on the relationship between parents and grandparents. If you find that your divorce has caused this kind of intense conflict between one set of grandparents and you, I strongly suggest you do not try to solve this problem by yourself. Get professional help.

Of course, this is a very extreme case. But in any divorce situation grandparents do tend to take sides. And when they do it is bad for you and it is bad for your children. So try to help the grandparents to be emotionally as neutral as possible.

Another potentially negative situation you may need to deal with, particularly if you use a grandparent as a full-time or part-time caretaker or babysitter, is a severe conflict between your ways of raising the children and the grandparents' ways. If the grandparents are flexible and easy to get along with, you will be able to talk out the differences in child-raising methods and to explain to them your views on child raising. If the grandparents are not easy to get along with and are very set in their ways, you may have great difficulty in talking over differing methods of child raising. In this case it might be helpful to say to the grandparent something like this: "Helen, I know we don't see eye to eye on raising children. So maybe it would help if both of us discuss this with a professional so that we could resolve some of our differences on how to handle Jennifer." If she will agree, then do it. If she will not agree, then you'll have to let that possibility go. If the grandparent is handling the children in ways that you think are really destructive (though this is very rarely the case), then as a last resort you may have to tell her you don't want her visiting the children any more.

With regard to helping the grandparent do the best possible job of day care and parenting with your child, I suggest you read up on how to put the grandparent on a positive reward system. You will find this in the chapter "The Positive Reward System" in my book *How to Discipline with Love.* Every time the grandparent does something you think is good with the children, be sure to praise him or her.

Apart from your and the grandparents' attitudes toward child raising, there may be enormous conflict between what grandparents think your life-style should be and what it is. The chances are pretty good that if they had their druthers, they would much rather you had a more conservative life-style than you do. But in some surprising cases, particularly if the grandparents are getting a divorce, you may find that their life-style is more jazzy than yours. What do you think of that? I can only say that no matter what their ideas are on your life-style, they have a right to have them and you're not going to change them. So don't try. The only point at which you draw the line is if they tell you how you should live. At that point you say, "Now, Audrey (or Billy), you certainly have a right to your own ideas on how I should live and if you were in my place you would no doubt live quite differently. But you are not in my Addidas, so please don't tell me how to wear them."

I have written this chapter as if both sets of grandparents lived in reasonable proximity to your family. But they may not. They may live hundreds or thousands of miles away. In this case, they can still be either positive influences on your children or nothings. You can help to steer them in a positive direction by suggesting ways they can relate positively to your children, for example, by sending the children postcards or tape recordings or by having them come to visit the children in the summer or having the children visit them. You will find a number of other suggestions for long-distance grandparenting in chapter 12, "Long Distance Grandparents," in my book *How to Grandparent.*

It's very important that you spend a lot of time and effort in relating to both sets of grandparents. They can either be great assets to your single-parent family or they can cause enormous trouble. Help them to become the positive assets that they potentially are.

The Stages of
Child Development

12. Infancy

In the next seven chapters I'm going to discuss the seven psychological stages of development that children go through from infancy to adolescence. I am also going to talk about what typically happens to a child if a divorce or the loss of a parent takes place at that stage. It is very important for parents to have this information. First, you need to know what your child is like at each different stage of development. Otherwise you will be in the dark as to how to handle her at that stage. For example, when your child turns two and enters what I call the stage of first adolescence (two to approximately three), she is going to be a very different child than she was from one to two. Typically she will become rebellious, cantankerous, and difficult to manage. If you don't know that this is a stage and that it lasts only about a year, you may conclude that your child is going to be difficult and rebellious throughout her childhood. And this is not the case.

Second, divorce or the loss of a parent puts enormous stress on a child, and you need to know how the typical child of each stage will respond to this stress. Otherwise you lack the understanding to help your child adjust to the situation.

Now I want to issue one important word of warning: The descriptions of the psychological stages and of the effect of divorce or death on a child at each of these stages are not to be taken as hard and fast rules. They are merely guidelines for each stage and for the impact of divorce or loss on that that stage.

A child's biological temperament has a great effect on what she is like at any particular time. My daughter Robin was a gentle angel in the difficult stage of first adolescence, while my older son Randy was a raging lion at that stage. So the description of the typical child at each stage is only a very rough guide to your own child. In the same way, when I describe the psychological impact of divorce and loss at each stage, remember that children vary enormously in their capacity to withstand stress.

I remember once when Randy was four and going through the "family romance" aspect of the preschool stage. I came home early one afternoon and was greeted at the door by him. He said "Go away, I want Mommy," and slammed the door. Since I was familiar with the family romance, I smiled at his vehemence. But if I hadn't known about the stage he was in and if I had also been a divorced father, I could have drawn all sorts of wrong conclusions from Randy's behavior: "Randy doesn't love me anymore." "He's chosen up sides and his mother has won." "I'm in big trouble with Randy." But my knowledge of the family romance prevented me from jumping to any of these wrong conclusions.

Furthermore, in describing these stages and the impact of divorce or death upon them I deal with only one child at a time. But in most families, there is more than one child, and the interaction of the children in their different stages needs to be taken into account. So with those notes of caution, let's talk about the stage of infancy.

Between birth and late adolescence your child goes through seven different psychological stages of development. In each stage the child must face and master a particular developmental task if she is going to proceed successfully to the next stage. The child climbs the psychological ladder of childhood by proceeding from one developmental task and one psychological stage to the next.

The very first developmental stage of childhood is infancy. This stage begins at birth and lasts until your youngster begins walking. It occupies roughly the first year of life.

The developmental task of infancy is to acquire a basic outlook on life. The infant will acquire a feeling of basic trust and optimism about life, or a feeling of basic distrust and pessimism, or something in between. She will learn to have a happy and optimistic view of life if her basic needs are satisfied. What are her basic needs? They are: (1) to be fed when she is hungry, (2) to receive cuddling and physical affection, (3) to experience a deep and fulfilling emotional relationship with her mother and father, (4) to be given sensory and intellectual stimulation to aid in her general intellectual development. If your baby has these basic needs met, then she probably will have a good sense of basic trust about the world. And her sense of basic trust will be a good foundation for succeeding stages of psychological development.

An infant feels the impact of a divorce only indirectly. She is, after all, only a baby. But the indirect loss may be considerable. For example, she may lose the nurturance and emotional support usually given her by her mother or father. In an extreme case, either or both of the parents may be so unable to function that they need to be hospitalized. Or one or both parents may have their functioning so impaired with the baby that they need to provide a substitute parent for a time, either a relative or a paid caretaker.

Almost inevitably, the quality of parenting is adversely affected by the stress on the divorcing parents. When this happens, the baby may not get the full amount of nurturing she needs to build up a sense of basic trust in life at this stage of development.

Obviously, there are many unknown factors which cannot be spelled out with accuracy in such a description. For instance, how disorganized is the mother or father by the divorce and to what degree is their nurturing of the baby impoverished? If the parents have to turn to a substitute parent for help, how warm and loving is this paid caretaker? Obviously, the answers to these two questions make a great deal of difference.

But one thing seems clear. If the parents are going through the stress of a divorce, they are quite unlikely to be able to operate at their predivorce level of nurturing the baby. To the extent that they cannot function at their predivorce level, the baby loses out.

The effect of a parent's death on a baby is different. Death not merely causes parental nurturance to diminish; it completely knocks out the functioning of one of the parents. (Total desertion by a divorced parent of course has the same effect.) There is no way this can be explained so that an infant can comprehend it. The baby is left with the awful and mysterious absence of one of her parents, and she has no way to conceptualize it. This is usually worse when the mother dies, because she is ordinarily the chief caretaker. But the death of the father is traumatic also.

What can you as a parent do to help your baby in these circumstances? You are in a Catch-22 situation. On the one hand, your baby needs nurturing, but you find it hard to do this since you need nurturing so much yourself. Your best bet is to try to find a professional who will counsel you and give you the nurturing and emotional support you need. This is usually expensive, but it's worth every penny when you are in such a state of crisis. If you live in a reasonably large city, you can usually find counseling scaled to your ability to pay. You may have to get on a waiting list, but it will be well worth it. Or you may find a priest, minister, or rabbi who has had some training in counseling and can help you by acting as a sounding board. Or you may find a good friend who can act as a sounding board for your troubles. But in any event you need to find some emotional help for yourself before you will be able to give your baby the support she needs.

What all of this boils down to is this: Get some help and emotional support for yourself so that you are able to function at a predivorce or predeath level of emotional nurturing with your baby.

13. Toddlerhood

When your baby first begins to crawl ⟨...⟩
the stage of toddlerhood, which lasts f.ɔm approximately the
onset of walking to the second birthday. The onset of walking
varies enormously among children. Some start as early as
eight or nine months; others begin as late as fifteen or sixteen
months.

Your toddler has taken a giant step forward, both figura-
tively and literally, from his baby days. In infancy he had a
passive stance toward his environment. Now that he can walk,
he has an active stance toward his world. He is the Young
Explorer. He explores everything he can see or reach or rub
up against or get his hands or mouth on.

In fact, it is your child's developmental task now to build his
self-confidence by exploring and learning about his world.
When he was an infant, his developmental task was to build
up a sense of basic trust in his world. This was passive learning, for the baby is dependent upon others to fulfill his needs
for food, cuddling, baths, and diaper changing. But the learning of the toddler is active, for he can explore his own world.

All your toddler needs to help him learn self-confidence is
simply the freedom to explore his world safely without hin-
drance. But if he is surrounded by a thousand no-nos as he
tries to explore, he will learn self-doubt instead of self-confidence. He needs his own special world in at least a part of
your house and yard which is accident-proof and full of things
to climb on and play with (including "toys" like pots and pans
and other medium- to large-size unbreakable objects). Then
his exploration and his learning will be conflict-free and will
build up his self-confidence.

In such a free environment your toddler will come to feel
"I can do many things. I can crawl and walk and run and jump

n pull things and haul them and bang on them.
ith sand and water. I can build with blocks. I can
cars and trucks and airplanes. I can play with words
unds and learn to love nursery rhymes and books." His
al development is encouraged by his "conversations" with
you and by his own explorations with words and sounds.

An enormous amount of learning is going on in your child
during this stage. The basic motivation behind all learning is
curiosity. And your toddler is learning to freely express his
curiosity. He tirelessly explores his world, carefully examin-
ing everything he can get ahold of. He is learning and perfect-
ing his large and small muscle skills. His imagination is ex-
panding enormously. His oral language development takes a
large leap forward. And in all of these activities he is learning
self-confidence instead of self-doubt.

In contrast to the stage of infancy, a child in toddlerhood
is directly vulnerable to the stress of losing a parent, whether
through death or divorce. This age child does not understand
exactly what is going on in his family. It's as if he sees what
is happening through multicolored lenses that distort the picture. But whatever he sees, he knows it is not good. He knows
his family is unhappy, and this makes him feel unhappy and
upset too.

A child's divorcing parents may act in ways that are especially upsetting. The mother and father may hurl verbal abuse
at each other or even physically abuse each other. The toddler
may see and hear awful scenes between his parents. His
mother may cry a lot. And even if the parents control their
outward actions, the toddler senses that they have terrible
feelings toward each other. In either death or divorce, the
toddler quickly discovers that his mother is less physically
available to him. It is certainly no secret to the child that
something terrible is going on, even though he cannot conceptualize what it is. But he certainly is aware that his parents
are not parenting him in the ways they did before.

So how does the toddler react to what he perceives? There
is no one set of feelings that all toddlers feel at this point. But
here are some typical feelings. His reactions are very primitive
and undifferentiated at this stage compared with later ages.
But they are still there.

Even though the toddler cannot differentiate clearly what is going on in his family, he feels scared and upset. He has taken for granted a world in which he had a mother and a father (and perhaps a brother or sister) who acted in certain ways. Above all THEY WERE THERE. Now that has changed. Daddy has gone.

It's hard for the toddler to picture just where an absent Daddy "is." To show you the primitiveness of the child's perception at this age, let me tell you an anecdote about my family. This concerns my younger son Rusty when he was in late toddlerhood. At that time I was going to appear as a guest on the Dinah Shore TV show. Rusty was familiar with the program, having watched it several times. I said at dinner casually to him, "Rusty, Daddy's going to be on the Dinah Shore show on TV tomorrow." As I said this I saw a look of fear cross his face. "What's the matter, Rusty?" I said. "You're gonna be on the TV?" he said. "That's right." "You're not going to be here in our family anymore? You're gonna be on the TV?" I suddenly grasped what he was think-ing. He thought that people on TV stayed somewhere on TV instead of with their families, and he did not want me to do this. It scared him, so I did my best to clear up the situation for him. So you can see how primitive a toddler's perception of his world is, and how strong his feelings may be about it.

The toddler with an absent parent worries about who is going to take care of him. His worries are very basic and physical. "Who is going to feed me? Who's going to protect me from robbers? If my mother and father don't like each other anymore, maybe they won't like me anymore either. If my Daddy is gone away, maybe Mommy will leave me too." The fear of losing his mother is the same whether his father's absence is due to divorce or death.

Up to the time of this loss the toddler was living in a world in which everything was in its place. The loyalty of Mother and Father to each other and to him was as secure as the existence of the big tree in the front yard. Now that has all changed. However the toddler may conceptualize it, he is experiencing a fear of abandonment.

The reaction of the toddler to the loss of the union of two parents is a deep feeling of sadness. He is sad at losing his father even if he was a father who saw little of the child or expressed little interest in him. In the case of a divorce, the toddler is preoccupied with fantasies of his parents getting back together again so he can once again belong to a happy family. But of course he has very little ability to verbalize these wishes or fantasies.

The toddler feels rejected by both his mother and father, but in different ways. He feels rejected by his father because the father has gone from the home. Even if the father is only divorced and sees him for visitation time, the little boy has no certainty that he will ever see him again. If the father's visits are sporadic and irregular, this tends to confirm the toddler's feelings that he will not see him again. If his father is dead it is difficult for him to grasp this and he keeps thinking he will somehow see him again.

The feelings of being rejected by his still-present mother are different. He knows that she does not pay the same amount of attention to him that she did before. Of course he has no way of reasoning that she has diminished attention for him because of her preoccupation with the events of the divorce or death and her own feelings. He feels that she doesn't pay as much attention to him because she doesn't like him as much, which is why he feels rejected.

Because of his feeling of rejection, the child feels very lonely. He misses his father and may feel intensely lonely for him. Even if the father paid little attention to him, the toddler creates in his mind a fantasy father who will spend lots of time with him and take him to the zoo and do many interesting things with him. If his mother has previously not worked outside the home and now has to work, he feels additionally rejected by her. He finds he is being taken care of by some strange women (or perhaps his grandmother), and he is very lonely for his mother. So the toddler feels that both of his parents in different ways are vanishing from his life. And he doesn't know what to do about it.

Few adults can appreciate the incredible effect the departure of the father from the home has on the young child. Like my son Rusty, who thought I was going to be somewhere inside the TV set, the toddler has great difficulty establishing where the father is in space. That's why a visit to the father's new lodgings, especially to stay overnight, is so important to establish in the child's mind just where his father is.

So with his divorced father absent, the toddler worries about him. "Where does Daddy live? What does he do? When does he get food to eat? Who will take care of him if he's sick?" These are not the sharply articulated worries of an older child; toddlers have their own kind of blurry, misty worries.

Toddlers worry about their mothers also. Since they have only one parent left they worry whether something will happen to her also. "What will I do if Mother gets sick? Who will take care of her? If she gets sick who will take care of me? Mommy cries a lot and I worry about what might happen to her."

We can see that although your toddler is not a very verbal person, a number of feelings are going on inside his mind at the time of the breakup of his family as he has known it. The antidote for these negative feelings is to spend time playing with your child, above all giving him lots of cuddling and close bodily contact. Now is when it is really important to spend quality time with him, time when he has your complete attention. It is terribly difficult for you to do this if you are struggling with a divorce or bereavement. But your child needs you, and your nurturance of him will, to some degree, help in recovering your own equilibrium.

14. First Adolescence

First adolescence begins at approximately the second birth-day and continues till approximately the third. While toddler-hood was a stage of equilibrium, first adolescence is a stage of disequilibrium. It is easy to tell that this is a stage of disequilibrium. When my younger son Rusty was in his stage of toddlerhood and you asked him to do something he didn't want to do, he would answer softly, "No, no." When he suddenly began answering "No, NO!!" I knew we had entered the stage of first adolescence.

Many parents call this stage the terrible twos. It is a descriptive-enough phrase, but I don't like it because it deals only with surface behavior. It does not get into the underlying reasons for the behavior.

First adolescence is very similar to the teenage years, which I call second adolescence. Both are transition stages. Teenage adolescence is a transition from childhood to adulthood. First adolescence is a transition from babyhood (the English call the toddler a "runabout baby") to true childhood. Since it is a transition stage, the child is more vulnerable to psychological hurts and more apt to act in an extreme form. The first adolescent is typically subject to temper tantrums, frequent changes of mood, and many outbursts of tears. He is also quite demanding. Everything has to go his way. It is hard for him to compromise or to adapt to what others want. For example, if by mistake you leave out a word when reading him a favorite story, he may throw a fit.

The developmental task of the first adolescent, like the task of the second adolescent, is to establish his own unique self-identity. It's important for you to know that negative self-identity precedes positive self-identity. In this respect too the first adolescent is like a teenager. A teenager may not have the faintest idea of what he wants. All he knows is what he *doesn't* want. He doesn't want to be like his parents in any way, shape, or form. He doesn't want to cut his hair the way they like it. He doesn't want to listen to the kind of music they like. He doesn't want to wear clothes that are like theirs. And so forth. He has to go through a stage of rebellion against his parents and all that they believe in and stand for. Then and only then can he find out who *he* is and what he stands for.

The first adolescent is going through a similar experience. Whatever his parents want him to do is exactly what he doesn't want to do. His favorite word is NO!

Not only is your first adolescent's behavior very negative, but his decision-making style can drive you up the wall:

Toby: "I want a glass of milk."

Mother: "Here it is, a nice glass of milk for you."

Toby: "No milk. I want orange juice!"

Mother: "All right, here's your orange juice. Now be satisfied!"

Toby: "No, I don't want orange juice. I want a drink of Coke!"

Mother: "#!*?#$*"

In many ways your first adolescent acts like the Little King of the family. His word is law. He is very domineering and delights in issuing orders to everyone. His ability to share, to take turns, and to wait is very limited. And he is constantly shuttling back and forth between his desire to move on to the maturity of childhood and his wish to regress back to the safety of babyhood. One day or even one hour he wants to become independent, and the next day or the next hour he wants to remain a dependent baby. He may indignantly turn down the offer of his mother to help him dress, with a scornful outburst, "I'll do it myself!" And the next time he will suddenly go limp and say, "Mother, you do it."

It's easy to see that even in a normal, happy family it is hard to manage a first adolescent. When you add to the family the extra stress of a divorce or an absent parent, the problems compound. Especially if the atmosphere is tense and hostile, as in a divorce situation. The first adolescent then is like a child running around with a chip on his shoulder. You need that like you need a hole in your head. You already have all the stress and difficulty you can handle.

In general, a first adolescent has the same feelings inside his head that the toddler does, which we discussed in the last chapter. But because of his stage of development, the first adolescent's feelings are much more easily set off and much more intense. The first adolescent is likely to attack you verbally, even physically (which you should not allow), when he is upset. In the case of a divorce, he may not understand that it's the divorce he is angry about, but he will get upset at you nevertheless.

What is the best way to handle your first adolescent in this situation? Part of the answer will depend upon how verbal he is and how much he can put his feelings into words. Some first adolescents are much more verbal than others, and you can encourage them to verbalize their feelings and you can respond to them:

Mother: "Tell me more about it, Jeremy. What is Jeremy mad about?"

Jeremy: "Daddy's gone away and Jeremy's mad."

Mother: "Daddy's gone away and you're mad about it."

This would be an unusually verbal first adolescent. Many would not be able to put these feelings into words. Others would express their angry feelings by hitting. Whether your first adolescent is verbal or nonverbal, it is wise to keep your restrictions on him down to an absolute minimum. Be as relaxed about making rules as you can. Having a minimum of rules for him to rebel against is always good advice for this stage. But it is especially wise when your first adolescent is going through the stress of a divorce.

Give your youngster as many outlets as possible for his anger: beanbags to throw, punching bags to punch, batacas to hit with (these are commercially made stuffed bags which cannot hurt anyone but which a child can use to hit with). You can also make some faces out of sturdy cloth and fill them with stuffing, and your child can punch them. As he punches, you can cheer him on. "That's it, Jeremy, hit that old face. Hit it hard!" Give him all the outlets for his angry feelings you can, but don't let him hit you or any of his brothers or sisters.

The situation is different with a first adolescent whose parent has died. His reaction will be mainly great sadness. Any anger that exists tends to remain at a deeper level of consciousness and is unlikely to be expressed. Except you may find that when he is tired or thwarted he becomes more angry or sulky than usual. You will want to comfort this child and help him to express his sadness. Encourage him to talk about what he is feeling, but do not force him. Let him know by your words and by cuddling him that he is loved and will be taken care of.

Generally speaking, life with a first adolescent is not easy even under normal circumstances. But when coping with him begins to get you down, think about what kind of an adult you would like him to grow up to be. For the very qualities that make him obnoxious and difficult to handle at this stage are going to help him become a dynamic, forceful adult. His dynamic quality is a very important psychological resource for him, even if he is more difficult to handle. So don't think of his dynamic quality as something to be eliminated from his personality. Think of it as a valuable asset.

15. The Preschool Stage

So far your child has had only one developmental learning task at each psychological stage. Now, with the preschool stage, she has nine developmental tasks. Here they are: (1) to fulfill her biological needs for development of both large and small muscles, (2) to develop a control system for her impulses, (3) to separate herself emotionally from her mother and become independent, (4) to learn the give-and-take of peer relationships, (5) to learn either to express or repress her feelings, (6) to establish her gender identity, (7) to form her basic attitudes toward sexuality, (8) to work her way through the "family romance," (9) to go through a period of being particularly responsive to intellectual stimulation.

You can see that a *lot* is going on during the preschool stage.

Compared with her earlier stages, your preschooler is quite sophisticated and poised. She is much more articulate, and you can actually hold a conversation with her. She will generally speak her thoughts and feelings freely. You will really enjoy having her around, after enduring her rasping personality as a first adolescent. This is the stage when your child is beginning to turn into a real person.

In discussing each of your child's developmental tasks as a preschooler, I will be speaking in broad, general terms. As I've said before, each child is different from every other child, especially in the degree to which they express particular aspects of themselves. But in addition to the differences among all children, there are also differences between boys and girls, which begin to show up more clearly during the preschool stage. For example, little boys tend to be more aggressive than little girls. And girls tend to mature faster in their language and emotional development. Again, this is a generalization. But these do seem to be gender-related differences, which your children themselves will probably demonstrate to you. We will talk about this more later in the chapter, when we discuss your child's development of gender identity.

So let's talk about the developmental tasks of the preschool stage.

Your preschooler is like a biological factory that takes in energy in the form of food and expends it by running, jumping, climbing, and yelling. It is rare that a preschooler simply sits still. But all of this activity is important to her. It helps her in her large muscle and small muscle development, which is her first developmental task at this stage.

Your child is also occupied with the developmental task of building a control system for her impulses. Of course she begins to learn rudimentary self-control in toddlerhood, but her control system is by no means fully developed until she is approximately six years old.

It takes much more time than most adults realize for a child to be able to say "no" to her impulses and keep them in check. When she is very young and sees an apple in the grocery store, she may immediately grab it. It is only later that she learns this is not socially approved behavior and can check herself. Since it does take a long time for a child to be able to say "no" successfully to her impulses, you cannot rush her. Think of learning to play golf and how long that takes. You need to learn how to drive, how to hit an approach shot to the fairway, and how to putt. Then you need to be able to put all of these skills together to play a good game of golf. It's the same way with all of the social skills that go to make up impulse control for a preschooler.

The next two developmental tasks are linked together. Your child needs to learn to separate emotionally from her mother and she needs to learn the give-and-take of relationships with her peer group.

When your child is a toddler or a first adolescent, she is still very much dependent on you. You are the fixed star of her existence. But by the time she is three, that situation has changed. She is now ready to launch off by herself and cut some of the psychological apron strings that bind her to you.

Your child is also ready to spend more time playing with

other kids and learning how to handle relationships with them. As her mother, you more or less accept her just as she is, because she is your child. But other boys and girls don't feel that way about her. They like some things she does but they don't like others. And they make no bones about telling her how they feel. At times they may even reject her and say, "Go home."

So your preschooler learns that her peers are very different from her family. It's a brand-new world, with different rules and different demands. This new peer world offers the child the opportunity to learn a new set of socialization skills she could not possibly learn within the confined circle of her family. She learns how to be self-assertive and stand up for her rights when some other youngster tries to take advantage of her. She learns how to share with others. She learns how to put her feelings into words. She develops self-confidence in relating to other children. These things she is learning between three and six are basic social skills that she will use throughout her life.

One of the best ways of helping your preschooler solve both of these developmental tasks (separating from Mother and learning to relate to her peers) is to send her to a good nursery school or day-care center.

In a nursery school, a child learns to get along with fifteen other children and a teacher who is at first new and strange to her. And if you want to see how BIG a step this is for a three-year-old, simply visit a nursery school on the first day of school and see all the children crying and being held on the teachers' laps. But your child learns there. She learns that you really are coming back at the end of the school day. And she learns to function without you—albeit with protests and tears. In so doing, she gets in touch with a tough core of independence within herself that is not always dependent on having Mother around.

I suggest you start your child in nursery school two days a week, increase to three days, and finally to five days. This gradual approach helps to ease the emotional difficulty of separating from you. Not only does your child learn how to function emotionally without you in nursery school, she also learns to relate to the other children in her class, who have quite different personalities and degrees of assertiveness than she does. When your child learns peer relationship skills in nursery school, she is way ahead of the youngster who doesn't begin learning such skills until kindergarten.

The fifth developmental task for your preschooler is to learn to express or repress her feelings.

Probably most of you parents were raised as I was. We were taught not to express our feelings to our parents or grandparents or any adults. I was not even allowed to disagree with my mother or father. If my mother said Milan was the capital of Italy and I said, "No, it's Rome," my mother would thunder at me, "Don't you dare contradict me, young man." Going further than that and telling my parents I was angry at them or hated them was absolutely verboten. I distinctly remember having my mouth washed out with soap several times for saying such absolutely terrible things.

If you were raised the same way I was, you may believe that children should not be allowed to express any negative feelings toward adults. Although you may have learned through psychology courses or books that it's good to let children express their feelings, still it may be hard for you actually to let them do it. It was certainly hard for me to learn to let my children express their negative feelings to me, their father.

Just about every psychological problem counselors come up against with their adult patients deals some way or other with the inability of the person to express feelings. So one of the best things you can do for your preschooler is to let her learn to express her feelings at this age. It will help keep her out of a psychiatrist's office later in life. Also, a person who can talk out her feelings will probably have a better marriage relationship and more rewarding friendships than a person who keeps her feelings bottled up. And a person who can assert herself and speak up to her colleagues will probably be more successful in her work than a person who keeps grievances inside and lets them fester.

The preschool stage is the most important time to give your youngster the opportunity to express her emotions, negative or positive. Of course no parent has any difficulty with positive feelings. It's the negative feelings that are the sticker. "Mother, you're great and I love you" is fine. But you may have some trouble allowing your daughter to say, "You're mean and awful and I hate you."

Consider this: Whether or not you allow your child to express her negative feelings, she will think them anyway. But if you let her get her negative feelings off her chest, positive feelings can take their place. Negative feelings that are not allowed to be expressed simply block the emergence of positive feelings.

At this point you may be wondering, *But what do I do when my child says these bad things to me? How do I handle them?* You can handle them by using the feedback technique I discussed in chapter 6. Allow your youngster to express whatever feelings she has of any sort: warmth, fear, anger, hurt, love. Then put these feelings into your own words. This shows that you truly understand. You may say things like, "You feel hurt because I gave your sister a piggyback ride and didn't give you one." "You're mad because I yelled at you."

This seems like such a simple thing to do. But it may be hard to put into practice at first. Just persist and you'll get the hang of it.

Please notice that I am recommending that you allow your child to express her *feelings* freely. I am not recommending you let her express her *actions* freely. It's OK for her to tell her brother she's mad at him, but it's not OK to hit him. Actions can get kids in hot water, but spoken feelings are just a communication. There's quite a difference between the two.

Your preschooler's sixth developmental task is to establish her gender identity.

When we talk about gender identity we are talking about the child's identification with the characteristics of one gender or the other. As we've said, in the preschool stage gender differences begin to emerge more clearly than before. Although males and females are both human beings, and although what they have in common is more important than what they do not have in common, little girls are different from little boys. Big girls are different from big boys. Adult women are different from adult men. These gender differences in no way imply that one sex is superior or inferior to the other. They are simply different. Unfortunately, in the past, gender identities have tended to become stereotyped into rigid roles, so that the fullness of the individual personality was prevented from emerging. Little girls were taught that they should be helpless and subservient, and they grew up to be women who were afraid to exercise their own independent natures. Little boys were taught that they should not cry or show their feelings. And they grew up to be men who were awkward and ill at ease in expressing their feelings.

Preschoolers are impressionable little people. It is unfortunate that they are presented with gender stereotypes just as they are in the process of developing their own gender identity. For such stereotypes emotionally handicap them as adults. These stereotypes are presented to preschoolers in books, on TV, in songs, and even, sad to say, by their parents. That's why it's important to read nonsexist nursery rhymes to your preschooler (such as *I Wish I Had a Computer That Makes Waffles*). And it's important to read nonsexist books to her, to let her watch nonsexist TV shows, and above all to talk to her yourself about men and women in nonsexist ways.

If you do this with your children, your little girl will still be different from your little boy, but she will not think of herself as being inferior to little boys. And your little boy will be different from your little girl, but he will not think of himself as superior to little girls.

If you accomplish this, your children will acquire their gender identities as boys and girls but they will be open identities, rather than closed and rigid ones.

Much of the learning of gender identities occurs through the imitation of role models. In the intact family, little boys model after their fathers and little girls after their mothers. But in a single-parent family it is different. A little girl can model after her mother, but who will the little boy model after? If the father keeps close ties to the children and sees them frequently, that may provide enough time together for the boy to model after him.

But what if the father is an infrequent, hit-or-miss visitor, or what if he is missing altogether? Then you will need to substitute, if you can, a male relative—a grandfather, uncle, or cousin—as a surrogate father who can spend time with the young child. Your boyfriends should not play the role of surrogate father with your little boy. It is not good for your child to have a succession of temporary father substitutes parading through his life. As I've said before, I would not let the children become really involved with one of your boyfriends unless things have reached a pretty serious point between the two of you.

Even if you have no male relative to provide a father surrogate for your preschool son, all is not lost. You can usually arrange to hire a male college student to spend a certain number of hours a week with your boy doing things that both enjoy: going to the zoo, playing games together, or visiting a fire station, police station, or newspaper plant. If there is no college nearby you can hire a mature high school boy to do these things with your preschooler.

Even though your child's loss of his father takes place during the preschool years, there are many things you can do to prevent this from harming the development of your child's gender identity. A gender identity is a very precious part of the personality. You want to make sure your youngster is strong and secure.

Your child's seventh developmental task is the formation of her basic attitude toward sexuality. Some of you may be surprised at this. "What? Attitude toward sexuality by six years of age? You can't be serious!"

Yes, I am. Of course I'm not talking about her attitude toward *genital* sexuality. I am talking about developing a healthy attitude about touching and body contact, which will become an important part of her adult sexuality. Unfortunately, many adults shy away from touching their partner nonsexually. A typical complaint of many wives is, "He never touches me except when he wants to have sex." But the preschool child who is hugged and kissed and fondled and stroked on the face and hair is being prepared for a full-bodied and warm sexual maturity as an adult.

In addition to letting our children learn to fully enjoy warm and affectionate body contact, our goal should be to give them the same positive or neutral attitudes toward their sexual parts that they have toward other parts of their bodies. Unfortunately, there are many ways in which children are taught that sexuality and their sex organs are "nasty" and should be avoided. For instance, mothers will typically delight in teaching young children the parts of their body: "Find your nose. Put your finger on your nose. Find your ear. Put your finger on your ear." But how many mothers proceed to say, "Find your penis. Put your finger on your penis," or "Find your vagina. Put your finger on your vagina"? What does the young child learn from this? She learns that her nose, hair, hand, knee, and foot are acceptable parts of her body. They all have names, and her mother is quite comfortable in using these names. But some of the other parts of her body must be bad. They are so bad they don't even have names.

How much more emotionally healthy it is when children know that their sexual parts are as acceptable as the rest of them. Like the little boy in the nursery school who spoke up to his teacher and said, "Teacher, my penis hurts. Something in my pants is pinching it." Wonderful! He was just as comfortable saying that as saying to her, "My foot hurts. My shoe is pinching it." Later on, at around age seven or eight, children become much more self-conscious and modest about their sexual parts. But an unembarrassed approach to the body during the preschool stage will be helpful to them as adults.

Amazingly enough, many married couples are unable to talk about their bodies to one another. They cannot communicate what gives each one pleasure and what doesn't. I have counseled a number of such cases. The couple may have been married for three or seven or nine years, but they do not have the courage to communicate their sexual needs to each other. Once they do learn to express what they want, their sexual and emotional lives improve greatly.

Amazing as it may seem, adult inabilities to discuss sexual matters stem back in the preschool years, when children quickly pick up the cultural taboos on talking about sex and the sexual parts of the body. I advise you to take deliberate steps to break these taboos. For example, when your little boy is having a nice warm bath, say to him, "Don't your legs feel nice and warm in your bath? And I'll bet your tummy does too. And so does your penis. It feels nice and warm in that bath." I'll bet you no other mother in your neighborhood is going to talk like that to her preschooler. But you will. And your preschooler as an adult is going to be able to talk more freely and naturally about sex than most other adults. And he is going to feel better about his body. This should go a long way toward helping him to be a good marriage partner.

I've suggested that you not parade a succession of father surrogates through your child's life. But when you do eventually form a close and firm relationship with a special man, he will be spending at least some time with your preschooler. It would be a good idea for you to educate him on the subject of preschool sexuality, just as you would talk to him about gender identity issues or other important tasks of your child's developmental stage. Without some background help from you, he might be at a loss as to how to handle your child's feelings or her questions on sex.

How do you handle a child's questions about sex? The ideal is to answer them as matter-of-factly as you would answer questions like "Why does it rain?" or "What makes a car go?" What I'm saying is, answer your preschooler's questions about sex as you would answer her questions about any other subject. Make your answers as simple as possible; you don't need to give detailed explanations. You will probably also want your preschooler to become gradually informed on the total subject of love and marriage and sexuality. There is a book that does an excellent job of this. It is called *The Wonderful Story of How You Were Born*, by Sidonie Gruenberg (Doubleday). It is a marvelous book with an interesting text and splendid illustrations that your child will love.

The eighth developmental task of the preschool stage is your child's resolution of what is called the "family romance." This is a psychological term for an ordinary but important developmental period. I'll describe it in terms of the boy first. Around the age of three a little boy falls romantically in love with his mother, and he continues to be in love with her until he is approximately six. He treats his mother in a special way and he wants her to treat him in a special way.

Please understand that this is not a genital sexuality he feels for his mother. It is more like the "crush" a young adolescent feels for a special teacher at school. Some little boys are quiet and private about their feelings. Others are more obvious: "When I grow up I'm going to marry Mommy." And then he may add, "And Daddy will go away somewhere and not come back." The phase of the family romance is very important to both little girls and little boys. During this phase the little boy begins to create a mental model of the woman he will one day marry. The little girl goes through the same process with her father. This "falling in love" with the mother or father is a very important precursor of the falling in love the child will do as an adult.

Ordinarily in a stable and happy marriage, the little boy finally decides that he is not going to marry Mommy when he grows up, because Mommy is already married to Daddy. He is going to marry another girl instead, but someone who is like Mommy. We even have a song about this: "I want a Girl —Just Like the Girl That Married Dear Old Dad."

If you have already married again by the time your child is in the stage of the family romance, then your new husband may well be cast in the role of the "romantic daddy" by your little girl. But don't let your boyfriend be cast in this role, for the relationship may end and your girl may find that her romantic daddy has vanished.

Don't poke fun at the romantic feelings of your son or daughter in the phase of the family romance. To you the feelings may be cute and humorous, but your children take them quite seriously. And they should. For what goes on at this stage of development prepares them for a future love relationship.

The ninth and final developmental task for your preschooler is to go through a period in which he is very responsive to intellectual stimulation. If your child gets a lot of intellectual stimulation during the preschool period, he will have a head start over other children when he enters school.

What kind of intellectual stimulation can you give him? First, you can read books to him. By reading books you are helping to develop his intelligence. You are teaching him to love reading. And you are building an excellent foundation for the reading skills he will acquire in kindergarten and first grade.

Second, you can teach your preschooler arithmetic and math through the use of the Cuisenaire Home Mathematics Kit (Learning Games, Box 520-C, North White Plains, NY 10603). Without going into detail on this, take my word for it that it's one of the most marvelous things you can do for your preschool child's intellect. Write in and inquire about it.

A boyfriend or a steady relationship may not understand either the delight or the importance of playing intellectual stimulation games with your preschooler. So you may have to educate him in how to do it. Both your child and your boyfriend will benefit.

There you have them—the nine developmental tasks of the preschool stage. You can see what a very important time of development this is in the life of your child. And there are many ways in which you can promote your child's intellectual and emotional well-being.

A child in the preschool stage is particularly vulnerable to a divorce or parental death. He can grasp what is going on in interpersonal relationships infinitely better than a child in the early stages. So if he sees the relationship between his parents dissolve into separation or divorce, he jumps to the conclusion that either or both of his parents might leave him. The result is that he is scared and sad. If a preschooler's parent dies, it is like a huge tree falling down in the forest. There is a terrible gap, which nothing can fill at first. This child too is very frightened and sad.

Like the preschooler whose parents are divorced, the bereaved child may cling to his mother when she leaves him on a routine trip to the store, crying and imploring her not to leave. Although he has previously adjusted well to nursery school, now he may greet his mother when she comes to pick him up with sobs or a temper tantrum. A child who has adjusted well to his mother's work outside the home may now find it very hard to let her go in the morning. And he may greet her when she comes home with the accumulated tension of a day in which he worried that she might not come back. Every departure of his mother becomes an occasion for worry and sadness.

Many preschool children of divorce or bereavement regress to earlier modes of behavior. They may have mastered toilet learning, but now they have "accidents." Outgrown security blankets become used again. The child's regressive behavior tells us that his feelings are too much to cope with. He has to regroup psychologically to an earlier time in order to withstand his current anxieties. Of course, when a child regresses, this puts an even greater strain on the mother to take care of him, just at a time when her own psychological reserves are at their lowest ebb.

Some children are very bewildered as they try with great difficulty to understand what has happened to their family. Sometimes they point to familiar objects in the home and ask their parent over and over, "What's that?" The object is a concrete representation of the absence of their other parent, and they are really asking, "What is this absence? What does it mean?" The play of many young children who are trying to sort out the meaning of a divorce or death centers around the theme of what belongs with what.

Many children of divorce take very personally the separation of their parents. They act as if the departed parent left because he didn't like them and is going to replace the children with another set of children somewhere else. It seems impossible for them to understand that the departure of the parent was directed at the other parent, not at them. A child may ask his mother, "Is Daddy going to get another Mommy and another little boy?"

Since many children are not able to have a clear conception of what is going on in a divorce or death (and the adults often do not help them see the scene clearly), they fill in the missing gaps with fantasies, often weird ones. These fantasies are created both by the child's limited capacity to understand the confusing events and by his own frightened understanding of the adult stress he feels around him. The common fantasy that preschool children express in their play is their fear of being left hungry by their parents. This of course is a concrete image of a fear of being abandoned. The children who are the most frightened are those who have not been given a clear understanding of what has happened to their family.

Fantasies are also used by preschool children to deny the reality of the father's absence from the family. The denial helps them to deal with their painful loss. Girls seem to use these fantasies about their father more than boys. In the fantasies of a little girl of divorce, the father is going to come back soon and love her and be with her. Many of these children say, "He loves me the best." Such a fantasy enables a child to deny the reality of the father's departure and her sense of rejection. A number of preschoolers show the impact of the divorce on their lives by increased irritability and hostility. They will express their hostile feelings to their siblings and parents, and at nursery school. Many children are not protected from witnessing parental quarrels or even parental fisticuffs. And these violent episodes may stimulate aggressive behavior on the part of the child.

The bereaved child too has fantasies and may tell other people that his daddy still lives at home. As with the child of divorce, his fantasies help him deal with the pain of his loss. As time passes and the child becomes more able to handle his feelings, the fantasies gradually fade away.

Many children feel guilt at the loss of a parent through divorce or death, especially a preschooler who loses the same-sex parent. For he is in the stage of "magical thinking" as well as the stage of the family romance. He may have wished that his father-rival would vanish. So when his father does leave, it is as if the child has caused it. This is true for both sexes —the little girl losing a mother would have the same added guilt feelings mixed in with her grief. In the case of a divorce, many children blame themselves in spite of explanations by their parents. These children may cling to their guilt and their self-accusations with dogged persistence.

Preschool children of divorce and bereavement often show intense hunger for love and affection. They will climb up on the lap of a strange adult and beg for affection, perhaps saying something like, "Timmy needs love."

This is a brief summary of the ways in which preschool children react to the loss of a parent. They need extra love and affection. They have great trouble understanding what is going on. In a divorce, they particularly fear their father will not come back. Preschoolers of divorce often show their feelings by becoming aggressive and hostile. It's important for the parents to make it as clear as they can that the divorce is like a fight between the parents that does not involve the children at all. And the parents should try not to take the heightened hostility of their children personally but to see it as the child's response to their anger at the divorce.

Wherever the divorced father lives, it's important for the

preschooler to see the father's home and spend a night there if possible, just as we suggested for the younger child. Many fathers have no idea how important they are to their children. The best substitute for a wild fantasy about the father is an interaction with a real father.

16. Middle Childhood

When your child was in the preschool stage, her family was her world. Even though she might have gone to nursery school and kindergarten, her horizons did not really extend much further than your family.

Your youngster broadens out in this new stage of middle childhood, which lasts from roughly the sixth to the eleventh birthday. In this stage your child occupies two new worlds besides the world of the family: the world of school and the world of the gang. Incidentally, your child's personality is pretty well stabilized in middle childhood. During this time, she does not have the dramatic ups and downs of the preschool period, when she might have been quite different at ages three, four, and five.

Let's take up in turn these two new worlds that are added to your child's life. First, the world of school. Up to the beginning of middle childhood, a youngster is generally accepted as she is by her parents. They do not make extraordinary demands that she change her personality suddenly in order to please them. In nursery school or kindergarten she begins to learn the social skills needed to get along with her peers, but now that she is in school, things are even more different. Now her acceptance by others is truly conditional rather than unconditional. She does not automatically get good grades; her grades depend on how well she does on tests and reports, in answering questions, and in classroom discussions. And the other students definitely sort out which students are average, below average, and above average in performance. Children may cruelly label a below-average youngster as a "retard." A child who is above average or extra bright often learns to keep a low profile, for she discovers that other kids may not like her if she is too smart. And woe betide the child, particularly a boy, who naively confesses that he "likes school"!

Children also sort each other out according to their sports abilities. A child may have a wonderful personality, but if he can't hit a baseball or jump rope, he will be the last person chosen. Kids also label each other's personalities. And if a child is labeled a "wimp," this will tend to stereotype the relationships of other children to her. Unfortunately, children with physical handicaps are also labeled in derogatory ways.

Children are capable of being quite vicious as they decide whom to let into their cliques and whom to reject. This is very different from the automatic acceptance and love your child found within her family during the preschool stage. In middle childhood, if she has a personality problem, if she is poor at games and sports, if she is too bright or not bright enough in her studies, she may end up being marked "thumbs down" by her peers. If this happens, you need to give her a chance to talk about it at home and offer her some emotional support.

Your child's developmental task during middle childhood is to learn *mastery* and avoid *inferiority*. This is the first time she has had such a task. For this is the first time she has had to compete with other children outside the family circle. She must master her schoolwork, physical games, activities outside of school, and the art of personal relationships with her peers as well. If she does not, she will feel inferior and inadequate.

One thing you can do with your child at this stage, if you enjoy it yourself, is to take her camping. Almost every girl and boy can learn to be a camper and to enjoy it. She can learn to pack her day pack, to set up a tent, to build a fire, and to cook meals. It will help your child's self-esteem as a whole to feel skilled as a camper. You can help her further by encouraging her in developing any of her other natural skills and by complimenting her on things she does well.

Now let's talk about the gang. At this stage of development "gang" means the peer group outside of school. This usually refers to neighborhood children. For your daughter, this means she will be spending most of her social time in the company of her girl friends, playing at whatever interests them. For your son, it is more likely to mean membership in a group with secret passwords and secret rules, even a secret name for the group.

Please do not think of the gang as some antisocial group of kids with switchblades. Not at all! We are talking about four or five eight- or nine-year-olds in a tree house. The activities of the gang could often best be described as "hanging around."

The members of your youngster's peer group are psychologically very important to him at this stage. He tries to conform in every detail to what they expect of him. In doing this he gains security by winning their emotional support and loyalty.

You see, your child's gang is the one thing in his life that is not organized by adults. It is *not* like Little League baseball, Pop Warner football, AYSO soccer, Cub Scouts, or Sunday school. The gang is organized solely by children. They want no adults involved in any way with what they are doing. If you want to read a classic study of what life is like in a gang of middle childhood, read *Penrod* or *Penrod and Sam* by Booth Tarkington. Many things have changed since the days of those stories, but the psychodynamics of life in the gang have not changed one iota.

The gang is a terribly important area of learning for your child. In the gang he learns valuable socialization skills, and they are entirely independent of adult supervision or evaluation. That's why they are so valuable. This is the first time your child has been able to venture out socially on his own.

Please don't think that because of the new importance of the world of school and the world of the gang, the world of the family has lost its importance to your child. The family is still very crucial to his existence. But he has an ambivalent attitude toward it. Dr. Barbara Biber sums up the paradoxical attitude toward the family at this stage in these words: "The child is looking for ways to belong to his family and feel free of them at the same time"("The School Years" in *The New Encyclopedia of Child Care and Guidance*, ed. Sidonie Matser Gruenberg, New York: Doubleday, 1968).

In middle childhood your son or daughter is still being powerfully influenced by her parents. She may often disobey your commands, but she is still underneath absorbing your attitudes, feelings, and values.

In other words, you are still the most important role models for your child. This will change drastically in adolescence, when the peer goup will become her most important role model.

The middle childhood youngster has taken an enormous leap forward emotionally and intellectually over the pre-school child. And increasingly over these years, your youngster's understanding about life matures. This means that particularly by about eight or nine, her understanding about a divorce or death will be very similar to your own: a realization that something final has happened, accompanied by both anger and grief.

During middle childhood your child's identity is closely tied to her family. You could say that her identity is organized around the concept, "I am the daughter of Howard and Bernice Jones." The loss of a parent, whether total or partial, can be a severe blow to her identity. For a child in transition from the world of the family to the much larger world outside, this is destabilizing. Her already shaky self-sense is made more insecure by the loss of her intact family.

Unlike the preschool child, who made considerable use of denial and fantasy to deny the family loss, a middle childhood youngster is often unable to muster effective defenses against her sadness. One seven-year-old child of divorce said, "I have to hold it in 'cause I'd be crying all the time." This child is very much aware that her wishes and fantasies for a reunited family will not come true. Another stated her true wishes: "First, that my Daddy would come home, second, that my parents would get back together, and third, that they would never ever divorce again." Then sadly she said, "It will never happen. I won't get any of my wishes." Like the preschool-age child, the youngster of early middle childhood (six to eight) is often full of fear and embroiled in many unrealistic fantasies such as the fear of being left with strangers or the fear of being left without a family. Fantasies of being deprived are widespread among these children: fantasies of being deprived of food, toys, or other things important to them.

In a divorce, the children are sometimes sharply shaken by the change in their parents' behavior. Previously they experienced their parents as guardians of their moral authority. They were told in no uncertain terms, for example, not to shout at their brothers and sisters. But now they experience their parents shouting at each other and perhaps using foul language. Their mother has told them, "Be good," but they now may observe her, a married woman (as they see her), running around with other men. They may see one parent spying on the other or lying to the other. These activities threaten the child's identity by assaulting her sense of right and wrong. Do the best you can to show your child that the value system you taught her is still intact.

Of great psychological importance to the children of this stage is the longing for the departed father. A little boy of divorce said, "Nothing feels right because Daddy isn't home." Boys miss their fathers much more intensely than girls. As in earlier stages, the intensity of missing the father has no relationship to the former degree of closeness between the father and the child. Very few boys of this stage express anger at their fathers. However, a boy who is in touch with his deeper feelings might express anger at his father for having died, although it is more likely that his anger would be directed at God or some other outside factor. In the case of divorce, boys sometimes are angry with their mothers for either causing the divorce or driving their fathers away.

The older children of middle childhood (nine to eleven) are distinguished from the younger ones by their ability to understand the implications of the sad event for their own lives. The feelings that usually bother them the most are their feelings of powerlessness and helplessness. In order to counteract these, children often try to take action of some kind. For instance, a child of divorce might embark on a campaign to pressure her mother to give up her dating and return to her father. Such activities, successful or not, give the child some relief from the feeling of helplessness.

For the older child, acting out her anger also helps obliterate her sense of powerlessness. In the case of a divorce, this might mean a tirade against the remaining parent, in the form of an adult-type scolding. In homes where the father has been harsh and punitive in his discipline, his departure might mean a new freedom for the child to express hostile impulses that have previously been held in check.

Any age youngster of middle childhood might unconsciously express her distress with disturbances of eating or sleeping, poor grades, or aggressive behavior. Rather than punishment, this child needs hugging and holding and reassuring that she is loved and will always be taken care of. Even without these nonverbal cues, your child needs nurturing now just as much as in the earlier developmental stages. As always, encourage her to express her feelings about the family crisis, using the feedback system to let her know you understand and accept what is going on inside her.

Unfortunately, middle childhood is also the stage in which children are mature enough for one or the other divorcing parents to try to enlist them on their side against the other parent. In spite of these emotional pressures and pulls, many children continue to be loyal to both parents. Frequently this is in secret and at the cost of considerable psychological suffering. Sometimes, however, a child will decide, "If my parents won't let me love both of them, I might as well get more love by siding with one of them."

These alignments of parent and child may be quite long-lasting. On the part of the parent, the purpose of an alignment may supposedly be to reunite the family, but the hidden agenda is usually revenge. The child who joins in an alignment is usually psychologically less stable and has lower self-esteem than a child who does not. The child in an alignment feels more needed, more important, and less helpless because she is playing an active role in the divorce. The children most likely to succumb to the lure of an alignment are the older rather then the younger boys and girls of middle childhood.

Needless to say, it is very detrimental for your child to feel pushed to align herself—or to be allowed to align herself—with either parent. She needs to be able to love both of you.

It is clear that your relationship with your child and your support and nurturing are extremely significant at each stage of her development. Even with your youngster's increased maturity and autonomy in middle childhood, she is still only a little girl, largely dependent on you for most of the important things in her life. During a crisis such as divorce or death, she may depend on your emotional support more than ever (although there are children who seem to sail through a family crisis or grow stronger in adversity).

Whatever your child's response to crisis, you can help her to provide some of her own emotional support now, in ways that are cheering to both of you. For example, she is mature enough to be much more of a companion to you than before and can converse with you about good and bad in the world of school and people. She can also help to make decisions about the running of the household and begin to carry out more grown-up duties. This does not mean that you are giving up any of your parental power. But you are letting your child participate in the family in more meaningful ways. This helps maintain her feeling of being important and needed, and it gives her a feeling of stability during the family's difficult times.

17. Preadolescence

For eleven years you have attempted to build good habits, attitudes, and values in your youngster. And you seem to have succeeded. Then, just as you are getting ready to congratulate yourself, he turns eleven. Suddenly, positive attitudes are replaced by negative ones. Love and warmth are replaced by hostility.

What has happened to your happy, gentle, easygoing ten-year-old? He has been hit by the growth forces of puberty and adolescence. These forces suddenly break out in the eleventh year, ushering in the stage of preadolescence. I will never forget how my daughter erupted into preadolescence. She was within two months of eleven when it happened. We had finished dinner one night and I asked her to take out the trash, as she had been doing for several years. But this time, to put it mildly, her response was different. "OK," she screamed. "IN THIS FASCIST SOCIETY THAT POSES AS A DE-MOCRACY, THIS FAMILY WHERE ADULTS HAVE ALL THE RIGHTS AND CHILDREN HAVE NONE, I'LL TAKE OUT YOUR BLANKETY-BLANK TRASH!" And that's the unique sound of the preadolescent baying at the moon.

The preadolescent can become quite obnoxious to live with, and girls are often as hard to put up with as their brothers. All of the good personality traits and attitudes he has acquired by long effort seem to have vanished. This stage covers the years from approximately the eleventh to the thirteenth birthday. It is a difficult stage for the child and an even more difficult one for the parent.

The developmental tasks of most of the other stages we have covered so far have been positive. But the developmental task of the preadolescent is *disorganization*. This is similar to the task of first adolescence, but at a much higher level.

121

Fortunately, it is not a permanent disorganization of the child's personality but a two-year turmoil leading to a new organization of the personality on a higher plane. Or you could put it a different way and say the developmental task of preadolescence is to wage a successful battle against puberty.

As part of the disorganization of personality of the preadolescent, the child's cooperation with his parents falls to zero on a scale of one to ten. You will make a reasonable request, such as that the child needs to wear a coat because it is thirty-four degrees outside. The preadolescent will respond as if your request were the most ridiculous and stupid suggestion he has ever heard. By the time you have endured a number of these rasping irritations on the simplest requests of everyday life, you are ready to climb the walls.

Up to age eleven, you were under the illusion that you had instilled some rules of elementary courtesy and values in your child. All these appear to have vanished. His conscience seems to have weakened, and his control over his antisocial impulses seems to have slipped.

Furthermore, the preadolescent knows just where to step on your toes where it will hurt the most. For a number of years, unbeknownst to you, he has been making a careful study of you. Now he puts the information he has gathered to use in his various antiparent sorties. He knows exactly which actions and attitudes will irritate the most.

For instance, if he knows that his school grades are very important to you, suddenly his grades will take a nose dive for no apparent reason. If you are uptight and moralistic, he will begin to specialize in telling jokes at the dinner table that would make a marine drill sergeant blush. I will never forget the imitations of me that my son Randy specialized in at the dinner table at this stage. "Members of the family, I will now lecture to you on how to be successful in life by following my example. Always work hard like I do. Always use big words when you speak, etc., etc." I must confess that I did not think the imitations funny, although the rest of the family found them hilarious.

It's important to realize that our preadolescents are not stepping on our toes only. We are representative of the whole adult society and the value system of the whole adult society.

The preadolescent needs to rid himself of adult society's value system in order to make progress toward his own individual adulthood. It's very important for parents to realize they are really innocent bystanders. I'll admit that when Randy was imitating me at the dinner table it was difficult not to take it personally. It was hard to remember that he was ridiculing the whole adult society, not me. I would say to myself, *I'm just an innocent bystander. I am! I am!*

So far I have written as if all of the changes taking place in your preadolescent were psychological in nature. That is not correct. The changes are also biological and physiological. Because underlying the behavior changes of your preadolescent are the powerful forces of puberty. Some parents even speak as though some mysterious force of nature has grabbed hold of their youngster and caused him to act in mysterious ways that cannot be explained by his day-to-day environment. "I just don't know what has gotten into him," the parent will say in bewilderment. When a parent speaks this way she's talking about puberty, even though she may not know it.

Of course parents cannot see puberty in their youngster. They can only see the outward manifestations of the sexual and hormonal changes taking place inside their child.

When your child was in the stage of middle childhood (ages six to ten), his biological system was generally in equilibrium. But when preadolescence arrives, huge biological and hormonal upheavals disrupt this equilibrium. Your child shows a definite increase in activity level. He reminds you of a human perpetual motion machine; he seems incapable of sitting still. He is continually on the move in some form: squirming, twitching, or twisting around. He is subject to volatile changes of mood, which he never used to have. Disappointment and hurt feelings are common, but anger is perhaps the most predominant of his negative feelings.

Parents need to be aware that the unpleasant qualities of the preadolescent—his belligerence, his defenses, his surliness—are expressions of his search for a new identity. And to find this new identity he must break away from the identity he had as a child.

The death of a parent at this stage of the young person's life can be quite devastating. The preadolescent is fully aware of the finality of death and of the enormity of his loss. Like the late preschooler, he will go through the same grief stages —denial, anger, sorrow, and ultimately acceptance—that you do. How he responds outwardly depends on his individual nature: His reaction could range anywhere from being totally grief-stricken to showing few outward signs. Since the grief process is aided by expressing feelings, the child who holds his feelings back would probably benefit by being helped to express them. For some children, however, this is so painful that they may need some sessions with a professional therapist or counselor in order to get their anger and sadness out.

The preadolescent in a divorcing family often has little trouble expressing his distress, and it is likely to be shown as anger. A divorce is a huge blow to the preadolescent, which he resents intensely. We have said that he knows just how to hit his parents at their weakest spots. And with the divorce there are plenty of weak spots. Much of his ammunition is given to him by his parents themselves. For example, he will hear his mother scream, "Well, you better try to find some woman who is frigid. You're such a lousy sex partner!" He saves up these remarks, and the next time he sees his father he has a magazine article cut out to give him. "Here, Dad, you better read this article. It's on how to deal with impotence." If the parents could keep their mouths shut about each other, they would be depriving their child of much of his ammunition.

What can you do to keep your sanity if your divorce comes in the middle of your child's preadolescence and you have a typically mouthy, rebellious youngster? First, try not to take his attitude personally. Try not to become defensive and angry and hurt. Instead, try to take a long-range view of your child's behavior. Remember that even in an intact family, he is not rebelling against you personally. He is rebelling against adult authority as a whole. And in the divorcing family he's not rebelling against you personally, but against the divorce which has hit him very hard. He does not hate his mother and father. He hates the divorce because it is pulling his mother and father apart.

Imagine you are walking along the street and suddenly an eleven-year-old you do not know runs up and screams at you,

"You are an ugly woman and I hate you. You're no good! No wonder your husband left you." You would be bewildered and amazed. But you wouldn't take it personally. So try to let it pass when your child says things like that to you.

Second, remember that this behavior is normal. Being obnoxious is one of his ways of demolishing his childhood identity so that he can create a new self-identity.

Third, keep in mind that this stage of development is shortlived. It's only two years, and two years isn't a lifetime (although sometimes it may seem that way).

Fourth, try to look beneath your preadolescent's distressing behavior to the tender feelings underneath. Your child seems to be expressing nothing but hostility. But in reality he is expressing love. He is saying deep down, "Mom, I love you. Dad, I love you too. I don't want to see you get this lousy old divorce. I hate it! I'm angry at both of you for getting the divorce. But the reason I'm angry is because I love you!" When you realize this, you get quite a different picture of your child's behavior. So just grit your teeth and hang in there awhile longer. And show him some of the love and compassion that he isn't able to show you. It may help get him through too.

The child of bereavement and the child of divorce both need special understanding and support from you.

18. Adolescence

Adolescence is probably the most difficult stage for parents to handle, whether in an intact or one-parent family. The main reason for this is that parents do not understand this stage. Most parents think of their adolescent as a child, only larger, and treat him that way. But the adolescent is neither a large child nor an adult. He is a special personality *in transition* from childhood to adulthood. This is the process that began in preadolescence, when your child was busy tearing down his equilibrium (and probably yours) in preparation for starting the move toward adulthood.

Furthermore, this is not a linear transition; it does not flow smoothly forward. It progresses three steps forward and then takes two steps back, before moving ahead again. This is what makes the adolescent so puzzling to the adult. The parent does not know where the adolescent is coming from or where he is going. Often, neither does the adolescent.

An anecdote from my clinical practice may make this concept clearer. The parent of a teenage girl was talking about her relationship with her fifteen-year-old daughter. She and the daughter were shopping for a new dress for the girl. The girl had narrowed down the selection to three dresses, and she asked her mother which looked best on her. The mother thought a minute and then said, "I think the blue one definitely looks the best." She was rewarded by an outburst: "Oh, Mother, you always try to dominate my life and tell me what to do!" Rebuffed, the mother lapsed into silence.

A few months later, the two of them were shopping for a pantsuit. The girl asked, "Mother, which of these suits looks best on me?" Remembering the previous episode, the mother decided to play it safe. "I'm sure you can decide for yourself," she said. "Oh, Mother," the girl cried, "you never help me when I need you!"

At this point in the telling of the anecdote, the mother threw up her hands and said, "What do you do with a child like that? I don't understand her at all!"

Actually, once you understand that the girl is a teenager, a personality in transition, it all becomes clear. She is midstream between wanting to be a child and wanting to be an adult. When she wanted to make her own decision, she was reaching out to the side of her personality that wanted to be an adult. She really did not want her mother to make the decision for her at that time, even though she asked for her opinion. But when her mother said to make her own decision, that's when she was wanting to be a child again. Once the mother understood her daughter's swinging back and forth, the whole sequence was understandable.

When you understand that your adolescent is not one person but two, his behavior becomes clearer. He is a child, but he is also an adult; and the two live on a perpetual seesaw. It is this feature that makes adolescents so vulnerable to the stress of a family breakup. We will go into this in detail shortly.

The developmental task of the adolescent is to form a new selfhood, a new ego identity separate from his parents. By the time the young person is roughly twenty-one or twenty-two, he will have become independent of his parents and family. He will stand on his own as an adult.

Since there are huge psychological differences between younger adolescents and older ones, I divide this stage into two categories: early adolescence (thirteen to sixteen) and late adolescence (sixteen to twenty-one).

In the years of early adolescence, the teenager is trying to answer the question "Who am I?" within the world of his family, and he is doing it in a rebellious way. But in late adolescence, he seeks the answer to this question within the larger area of his society. He also makes two very important choices at this time: the beginning choice of a vocation and a choice of sexual and affectional relationships.

In early adolescence, with the arrival of puberty, the teenager must adjust not only to changes in feelings due to changes in life-style and sexual feelings; he must also adjust to a changing body. A body very different from that he had grown accustomed to as a child. He now thinks himself too fat or too skinny, too thin-faced or fat-faced, too tall or too short. These kinds of self-perceptions make many adolescents feel inadequate or socially inept. While you may think your teenager is quite good-looking, he does not feel that way at all. This is why he stays in the bathroom so long, studying his face zit by zit, not particularly pleased with what he sees.

Your youngster's bodily changes are due to the beginning functioning of the sex glands. Although there are enormous variations among teenagers, girls usually begin puberty earlier than boys. The newfound sex urges scare the daylights out of both girls and boys. But neither will admit to being afraid.

Girls whose sexual development and body growth come either very early or very late often have more problems in dealing with the changes. The girl whose maturation begins early finds that her semiadult contours set her off from her friends. She may have guilt feelings about the new and strange sexual feelings she discovers inside. On the other hand, the girl whose puberty comes particularly late has her problems also. She cannot understand her friends' suddenly increased interest in boys. She tends to feel estranged from her girl friends.

Early sexual maturation does not typically upset boys as it does girls. One reason is that a boy's body changes are sometimes less traumatic than are a girl's onset of menstruation and new contours. But for a boy, late maturation can be upsetting when other boys tease him about not being into sex yet.

In addition to having to adjust to new sexual urges and a changed body image, the young person now begins to work toward freeing himself from emotional dependence on his parents.

The key to understanding adolescence is the swing back and forth between the urge to become independent and the desire to remain dependent and childlike. Since your child has spent his entire life with you, it is not surprising that it is extremely hard to break away.

The most typical way of breaking away from parents is to revolt against them and seek out their flaws. But the adolescent is still too insecure in his self-confidence to be able to stand by himself emotionally as he cuts his old ties. His peer group gives him the emotional underpinning he needs to do this.

There is a sturdy idealistic stranger in most adolescents. Parents who see their young persons as "totally selfish" are missing the idealism, which is a crucial element in a teenager. It is an endearing quality, one you should pay attention to in your youngster, because it's something about him you can really enjoy. For example, a new concern about social problems and what he can do about them may develop. This idealism can also cause problems when he uses it to condemn something you have done that you see as normal but he sees as less than honorable. Such as telling a lie to avoid a social obligation, saying one thing and believing another, or padding an expense account.

Fifteen is the typical age when your adolescent tries playing the role of amateur psychologist. He zeros in on the personality traits of both teachers and parents. He is trying to figure out why people behave as they do. If his mother and father are getting divorced, this is a psychological gold mine for him. His observations on their behavior are often devastatingly accurate. Of course, he will steadfastly say that he is making these observations out of love and concern for his parents' welfare. A little hostility perhaps? Heavens, no!

One of the things parents of teenagers find hard to face is that their youngster is no longer a "neuter" but a highly charged person full of romantic and sexual feelings. Many parents regard their child as a neutral being. Now suddenly, with the advent of puberty and adolescence, they have to cope with a son or daughter who is no longer neuter but intensely sexual. It's not an easy thing to shift your parental point of view 180 degrees.

If many parents were to say their secret thoughts aloud, they might go something like this: *I worked hard to give my child the good things of life, and what thanks do I get? Our house is just a place where he eats and sleeps and talks endlessly on the telephone. And when he's not talking to his friends, he's finding fault with us. After all we've done for him, how can he treat us this way?*

Incidentally, you have undoubtedly noticed that talking on

the telephone (usually while listening to music) is your adolescent's favorite indoor sport. Talking with his friends is one of the primary ways in which he learns about human personality and social relationships.

It is in adolescence that unfortunately drug use rears its ugly head, if it hasn't already done so. I want to talk about this now. When we speak of drugs, I mean psychoactive drugs, which alter the mind in some way. Now let's define a drug experimenter, a drug abuser, and a drug addict.

A drug experimenter is a person who has tried one or two drugs and then given up. I would guess that about 90 percent of youngsters experiment with drugs in this fashion sometime during their teen or preteen years.

A drug abuser is a person who has gone beyond mere experimentation and uses drugs in order to meet psychological needs. His drugs are a chemical crutch. Sometimes, when a teenager is terribly upset by family trauma such as divorce or bereavement, he will turn to drugs to enable him to temporarily avoid facing his problems. The "low" of his life situation is replaced by the "high" of drugs.

An addict is a person who uses a drug that produces physical and/or emotional cravings that the person cannot resist. Heroin is a classic example of such a drug. Cocaine can be another, once the initial experimentation stage is past.

I think that parents need to be very concerned about a teenager who is abusing drugs or is addicted, but not about casual experimentation. It needs to be made very clear to
your youngster that you do not approve of drug use, however.

Adolescents experiment with drugs out of curiosity, out of wanting to go along with the crowd, out of seeking new sensation, and because drugs are available. Adolescents turn to reliance on drugs because there is a "hole" in their personality, a fault in their self-esteem.

The most important thing you can do to prevent your teenager's becoming a drug abuser is to raise him so that he has a psychologically healthy personality. Here's how you do that:

First, the strength of your relationship with your child is one of your best safeguards against future drug abuse. If your child has a deep, strong, loving relationship with his parents, chances are good that he will go through a normal rather than an abnormal rebellion in adolescence. Drug abuse is one symptom that the rebellion of the youngster has passed the normal point.

Second, you can help keep your adolescent from becoming a drug abuser by maintaining an open connection during all of his teenage years. This connection can be difficult to preserve, but it is important to achieve if you can.

Third, you can help keep your child from becoming a drug abuser by being sure that he has sound, accurate information about drugs during his preteen years. Read the information and become informed yourself, so that you can discuss it with him. Too often a youngster's drug knowledge comes only from his ill-informed peers or a biased source. Accurate information that he knows is true will help him evaluate what he hears from other sources.

But what do you do if you realize your child has become a drug abuser? I think this is such a serious problem that you should not try to handle it by yourself. Consult a psychologist, psychiatrist, or psychiatric social worker. You might have to drive a hundred miles if you live in a rural area, but do it. Since drug abuse is caused by something lacking in the self-esteem of the teenager, it is important to have professional help.

Now that we have talked about the abuse of psychoactive drugs, let's discuss that other drug, alcohol. While alcohol affects the mind as well as the body, it is not commonly thought of in the same ball park as the other drugs we have mentioned. Perhaps that's because alcohol is legal for adults to use. Some parents, strangely enough, are concerned about drug abuse but are indifferent to what alcohol can do to their youngster. They overlook the addicting quality of alcohol and the irrationality of someone, adult or teen, who has had too much to drink. Teenagers tend to overdo something that is fun and "kicky," like alcohol. Liquor and teenager are a dangerous combination, particularly when an automobile is involved. I know a teenager who was driving at high speed coming home from a party dead drunk. He drove off the side of the road and hit a tree. He totaled the car and it's a wonder he did not kill himself or someone else. We have all heard stories of teenage alcohol-related accidents.

Your best insurance against your child's involvement with alcohol or other drugs is to focus on developing a strong and loving relationship with him, and to help him develop a sense of his own worth. For drugs and liquor, after all, are only a pitiful chemical substitute for your love. They are also a crutch for someone who has not yet learned to stand on his own feet.

When we come to the sexual behavior of the adolescent, we find that things have changed drastically in the last twenty years. Sex has become much more open and free. Parents may like that or dislike it, but it is a fact. Dr. Robert Sorenson's study of adolescent sexuality in contemporary America (*Adolescent Sexuality in Contemporary America*, New York: World, 1973), which is a most comprehensive national study of the sexual behavior of American teenagers, brings us up to date on that subject. He says, for example, that 52 percent of all thirteen- to nineteen-year-olds in the United States have had sexual intercourse before they are twenty. Nearly 40 percent of the first intercourse experience takes place in the house of the boy or girl involved, and another 40 percent takes place in an automobile. Among nonvirgin adolescents, 71 percent of the boys and 56 percent of the girls have had sexual intercourse by the age of fifteen. Only 5 percent of the nonvirgin boys and 17 percent of the nonvirgin girls wait until they are eighteen or nineteen to have intercourse for the first time.

The study also shows that a strong minority of adolescents still cling to older sex dictates. Twenty-one percent of adolescents do not have sexual intercourse nor even engage in beginning sex activities. As a psychologist, I cannot tell you what ethical, moral, or religious stand is right for you to take. We live in a pluralistic society of ethical and religious beliefs. We Americans have no consensus on sexual matters, and we might classify parents into four attitude groups. This applies to parents both in intact and in single-parent families.

The first are those who strongly believe that sex should be reserved for marriage. As you can tell from Dr. Sorenson's study, only a small minority of adolescents actually live that way.

The second are what I call the ostrich or head-in-the-sand group of parents. They have a pretty good idea of what their teenagers are doing, but they put their heads in the sand and hide the knowledge from themselves.

Third is a realistic group of parents. They say, in effect, "I think you as a teenager will be better off if you wait until you are more mature to have intercourse. But we think an unwanted pregnancy is a bad thing, so we want to give you full information about contemporary birth control. We don't really approve of your having sex, but if you are going to have it, we want you to protect yourself."

Then there's a fourth group of parents with this attitude: "When I was a teenager everything was hush-hush. I got absolutely no education on sex at home. And I did a lot of things my parents didn't know about. I felt guilty, and I was frightened a lot of the time. I don't want you to go through the same turmoil. I hope you have a deep, caring relationship with a person before you become physically intimate. I also want you to marry and have a happy and satisfying marriage, including a good sex life. One of the dangers I want you to avoid is an unwanted pregnancy, whether you are married or unmarried. And that's why I'm going to give you birth control information.

"Another very important thing I want you to avoid is AIDS. We know very little about AIDS scientifically but we are learning more all the time, and most of what we know is bad. We know that everyone who gets AIDS dies. There are no recoveries.

"We know that AIDS is contracted by sexual relations and contact with the bodily fluids semen and blood. The only way to be safe from contracting AIDS is to use a rubber condom for intercourse. If you have sexual relations with a person who has sex with a number of different people, you increase your chances of getting AIDS. The safest kind of sex is to confine your sexual relations to one person you know is healthy.

Since we know relatively little about the AIDS virus, research on AIDS is going on around the world. You can keep abreast of this important research by reading pamphlets, booklets, and the latest material that should be available at libraries, hospitals, medical centers, and free clinics."

These diverse parental attitudes are conveyed in a thousand different ways, both verbal and nonverbal.

The findings of Dr. Sorenson about sexual behavior among adolescents may be disturbing to you. You may wish fervently that you were back in the days when parents did not have to cope with such sexual freedom of their children. But wishing will not set the sociological clock back. This is the way adolescents are today, and you will need to face up to it and do the best you can.

It may seem difficult for you as a single parent to know how to deal with some of the realities of your teenager's world. This is where your support groups can help. You and the other parents can exchange ideas and perceptions and give each other the insight and encouragement you need.

So this is the picture of your adolescent: confused and confusing, sometimes delightful but more often rebellious, a full sexual being, with possibly a touch of drugs. Difficult enough to handle in an intact family and sometimes even harder in a one-parent family.

For an adolescent, the death of a parent is a tremendous loss. Your young person's response to the bereavement will depend on the degree of maturity she has reached. If the death occurs during a time when she is rebelling and estranged from the parent, the guilt, rage, and sorrow can be overwhelming. If the parent dies after the young person has made her major personal adjustments, then her reaction will generally follow the same pattern as yours, in perhaps the same time frame, leading to a gradual resolution and acceptance. Your adolescent may be a helpful presence to you if you can share your mutual feelings. If she isn't able to do this, however, you must respect the privacy of her feelings. Perhaps later, when she is feeling more confidence in herself as a separate person, the sharing can come.

An adolescent needs the steady and supportive presence of her parents during her stormy years, and a parent's death pulls one of her main props out from under her. You may find yourself the recipient of twice as much helplessness, or twice as much testing of limits and other behavior through which she is actually trying to define herself. As with all other actions of your teenager, when these episodes are finally past, you and she can come out the other side as friends, even though you will always still be Mother.

A set of divorcing parents is of course very disturbing to a teenager. As with the bereaved adolescent, she misses the firm psychological base that two parents provide. She needs to return to home base from time to time to stock up on emotional supplies that are temporarily exhausted and to gather courage for her next venture with independence.

In a divorcing family the parents are emotionally deprived and cannot offer a secure home base for their child. This generates an intense anger in the adolescent, who feels bitterly let down by her parents. The divorcing also leaves a large gap in the control structure of the parents. When you and your spouse are preoccupied with your own problems and with getting your lives back on an even keel, your adolescent may be left feeling vulnerable to her own feelings and impulses. One thing she needs is strength and fairness from her parents when she is about to go off the track. This, of course, is the same with the adolescent who is bereaved. The need for the parents is there, but the parents cannot be fully present.

Another painful issue between an adolescent and her divorcing parents is the new perception of them as sexual beings. Ordinarily an adolescent regards her parents as sexless. But with divorce, all that is changed. As a seventeen-year-old girl once said to me, "For years my mother has told me to keep myself pure and blameless. You know what she said to me last night? She said she had missed out on a lot of sex while she was married and now she's going to make up for it. I almost fell off my chair. I told her, 'Mother, I don't want to hear any more about it!' "

Divorced parents sometimes appear to their adolescents to be in pursuit of their own pleasure, and they may even make their adolescent a confidant of their adventures. This can fill the young person with anger, to see parents who are satisfying their own needs but have little to give the young person as a stabilizer and role model. The parents' sexual freedom can be especially upsetting if the child has been brought up to see her parents in a different light. She may suddenly view them as hypocrites, who have abandoned all of the standards they set up for their children.

A divorce during the adolescent stage is the hardest for both parents and children to handle for several reasons. Some of these apply in part to the bereaved family as well.

One aspect of parental sexual behavior that adolescents, particularly adolescent girls, find particularly upsetting is to discover that their father is going around with a much younger woman. Especially if the much younger woman might not be too far in age from the male or female adolescent. It is wise to try to take an emotionally neutral attitude toward the father's behavior in a situation like this. If you join with your teenager in condemning the father, then you are making it difficult for him or her to use the father as a positive role model. You might say something like this: "Well, it's not strange that a father is as shaken up by a divorce as a mother and he would turn to a younger woman to reaffirm his masculinity."

Parents of all families tend to have the most trouble handling their teenagers, and this trouble can be worse after a divorce. First, the parents have usually raised the child with some form of punishment. When she becomes a teenager, punishment no longer works. The parents are in trouble if they haven't developed other ways of helping to keep their young person more or less in bounds.

Second, teenagers have much stronger egos and are able to stand up to their parents more than in earlier stages.

Third, the teenager is going through a difficult stage of rebellion at this time. When you add the situation of a divorce, rebellion against the parents goes up to the ninth power.

Fourth, the teenage stage is one in which there is more possibility of a parent's getting the teenager to gang up with him against the other parent. If the young person resists taking sides, she is using up huge amounts of psychological strength to do so.

Usually it is one of the parents rather than the adolescent who initiates taking sides. It is a terribly destructive thing to the adolescent to be roped into taking sides. It robs her of the freedom to love both parents during a crucial part of her adolescence. So if you resist any temptations to get your teenager to take sides, this will be a very important gift you give her. If the father lines her up to take sides, there is really nothing you can do about this. Don't try to fight it. Just be yourself and wait for her to change her attitude toward you. Ordinarily she will change her attitude in time.

The reverse of taking sides is the adolescent who tries frantically to get you and your husband back together. She will use all kinds of arguments and promise anything to try to accomplish this. It may be very tempting to think seriously of getting back together because it would make her so happy. But this would be a huge mistake. You should only get back together if the two of you decide, after due time, to come together for yourselves.

Fifth, the parents are seen as hypocrites by the teenager because of parental short tempers, petty behavior, and sexual activities. What the parents formerly punished, they are now doing themselves. This greatly damages the moral authority of the parents.

Sixth, your adolescent may feel that it was your behavior that caused the divorce and blame you bitterly for the breakup. You will be tempted to defend yourself and point out rationally that you were not the one responsible for the divorce. Rational analysis will do you absolutely no good in this situation. The only thing that will help you is our old friend the feedback technique. Here is how to use it with a teenager who is in a bitter tirade against you.

Gail: "Mother, I've been giving a lot of thought to this and I can see pretty clearly now that the whole responsibility for this divorce is yours."

Mother: "You feel I'm responsible for the whole thing?"

Gail: "Yes, I do. I've been talking to Dad about this and he felt I was old enough to understand the real reasons for the divorce." (At this point you may be wondering if it's true that the taste of cyanide cannot be detected in very strong coffee and thinking perhaps you could invite your husband over for a friendly cup to resolve some matters.)

Mother: "So you feel you've gotten a lot of enlightenment from your father about the reasons for the divorce."

Gail: "Yes! And it makes me furious to think of the terrible things you did to him. He says that never once in the years you were married were you emotionally supportive to him!"

Mother: "So he feels I didn't give him any emotional support at all."

Gail: "That's only part of it. I probably shouldn't tell you this, but he said you were sexually frigid most of the marriage."

Mother: "So he says that even in sex I struck out. Well, from what you're telling me, it seems clear you feel I was the main person responsible for the breakup of our marriage. This is how you feel now. You may feel differently in the future. I don't know. But I do think it's important that you and I can continue to talk this over and show our real feelings. And I think it's good you have shown me the courtesy of showing your real feelings today."

From this example you can see that the mother did several very wise things in talking with her daughter. First, she did not defend herself in any way. If she had, the daughter would only have argued more strongly for her position.

Second, she did not argue with her daughter. Argument is of as little use in a situation like this as trying to defend yourself against a cannon by holding up a newspaper as a shield.

Third, she praised her daughter for being able to express her real feelings at this time. Other than this, all the mother can do is to wait for the daughter's feelings to change in time and not try to force her daughter to change her feelings in any way.

Of course, all these things are not found in every divorcing family. But enough of them are found in the average divorce that they make it difficult for a family to survive without great turmoil.

The immediate reaction of a teenager to divorce or bereavement can range from catastrophic to maturing. Some young persons retreat into their shells. Some let their feelings run wild. Some are full of guilt and depression. Some continue along without showing much feeling at all. Some suddenly seem to grow up.

After a time, the turmoil smooths out and things return more toward normal. If your young person has a severe reaction to the family breakup, or if she continues to overexpress or withhold her feelings, even after several months have passed, get her some professional counseling to help her regain her equilibrium and strengthen her self-esteem.

The New You

19. Discovering the Hidden You

You may wonder about the title of this chapter. You may think, *What is the "hidden" me, and what does it have to do with me as a single parent?*

When you were born your personality was a gold mine of potentialities which has never been explored. As you grew up, many facets of your personality developed. When you married, your personality changed in response to your husband's personality.

Some years ago I counseled a forty-two-year-old woman who had been married sixteen years. Her husband saw me once and then refused to come anymore. This woman loved movies, the theater, and concerts. Her husband detested them. The only thing he liked was to go out to dinner—but not an exotic dinner, such as French, Japanese, or Moroccan. Just a good, solid American dinner like steak or prime rib. Their entire recreational life consisted only of going out to this one kind of dinner. And we don't need to go on to all the ways in which he hurt and belittled her, but he did.

After two years of therapy, she decided she could no longer live with this rigidity. Her husband was not attempting to be less rigid, and she decided she had better get out of this miserable marriage. As soon as she separated from him, she started on a veritable orgy of going to movies, the theater, and concerts. She was so happy when she told me about it: "I feel like I haven't really had a chance to be myself while I've been married to George. And now I can for the first time in sixteen years."

This may be an extreme case, but to some extent all of us tailor our personalities to our spouses. Here are some examples: You are married to an alcoholic. Consciously or unconsciously you squeeze your personality to fit his difficult life-style. Or you are married to a workaholic—he's devoted to the Great God Work. Since you can't share the main part of his life, you have to create interesting lives for the children and yourself.

Or let's say you are married to a passive man who comes home every night and settles down to watch television. Sometimes you feel like screaming, "Let's do something more interesting than watching that damn tube!" But you don't want to make waves, so you take your seat in the family room and pretend to be a part of the happy family watching television. And so it goes. If your husband frowns on something, you don't do it. The result is that many parts of yourself are not developed. This is one reason psychologists find that most people develop only one third of their true personality. This is not true of everybody, of course. But it's true of most people.

Now let me sketch a different picture of you. You are brimming over with enthusiasm for everything you do, and you have no fear of trying new things. You are gutsy and outgoing. You are devoured by an intense curiosity about the world and want to learn all you can about it. You can express all of your feelings. You can give and receive love. You have solid self-esteem and an attitude that lets you attack new projects with gusto.

You may say, "No, that's not me, but I sure wish it could be." Well, surprise! There was a time in your life when this was a true picture of your personality. When you were a toddler, only a year or a year and a half old, that's what you were like.

All toddlers have these personality characteristics, including you. So what happened? Parents, relatives, neighbors, schools—that's what happened. They ganged up on you and you allowed them to make you only a shadow of the you that could have been.

The toddler is not afraid to be who she is. But you as an adult, if you are like most people, *are* afraid. Since childhood you have been trained to adjust your personality to other people. What a shame!

Look at it this way. Your fingerprint is different from the print of every other person on this planet. And your real personality is unique and different from every other person on earth. The aspects that have not yet been allowed to fill in are *the hidden you*—the wonderful and exciting you that *can* be!

Here is another example. I was counseling a woman in her late forties. She had just separated from her husband and was in the process of divorce. After I had seen her for about three months, she came in one Monday and announced she was going to take up oil painting. She had never done anything like that before, but she had always longed to do something creative. Now she finally felt she had the freedom to do so. Over the next months she took art lessons and spent most of her free time painting pictures of the ocean. Then she joined a book discussion group and began to meet new people. And she enrolled in an art history class. At a certain point she felt she didn't need to see me anymore, since she was launched in the direction she wanted.

Three years later I happened to run into her in a department store. Gone was the drawn face she had when I first met her. Her face was happy and glowing now. She had remarried, and she told me proudly that she still kept up with her art. Now she was painting many things besides the sea. "I have you to thank for all this," she said. I corrected her. "No, you have yourself to thank."

When she was married to her first husband, she limited her personality. After her divorce, she allowed it to blossom.

What does this mean to *you*? It means you shouldn't make the mistake of trying to rebuild exactly the same personality you had before the hurricane hit. Your personality is much bigger than that. You are full of much more potential than you have ever realized.

So what do you do now? TRY NEW THINGS! The emotional support groups I suggested earlier in this book can be two of the new things you'll try. Don't say to yourself, "I've never done anything like that before. I just know I can't do it." Nonsense! Try it! Say to yourself, "The worst thing that can happen is that the support group won't work, but I won't be any worse off than I am now."

Join other groups you may have been mildly interested in but never did anything about: a photography club, a camping club, a gym, a dance group. If some of these turn out not to be your cup of tea, drop them. But you will enjoy others and they will help you bring out hidden parts of your personality.

Then there is sex. Talk about the hidden parts of your personality! As a counselor, I have heard many people, mostly women, say, "Listen, I never knew what sex was all about until I got my divorce." For example, a woman had been giving in only reluctantly to her husband's advances for years, and refusing his requests for experimentation. What she didn't realize was that she wasn't really rejecting sex and experimentation, she was rejecting her husband's manner, which was abrupt and unfeeling. When she later had a relationship with a man who was gentle and considerate, and who also wanted her to experiment sexually, she found she liked it.

Let the motto of your new life be: EXPERIMENT! EXPERIMENT! EXPERIMENT! Keep your mind free and open. Try anything and everything as long as it is not illegal, immoral, or fattening! If you can afford it, let a counselor, psychologist, psychiatrist, or psychiatric social worker be your guide to the emergence of your real self. See this person once a week if you can, or only once if that's all you can afford. You'll find it much easier to discover your potential self.

I am perfectly aware that many of the suggestions I am making are not easy. It takes courage to go a giant step forward, where you have never gone before. But it can be done and it can have happy results. I know. I have done it myself.

When I was fifteen and in my second year of high school, a friend talked me into taking journalism instead of English. He persuaded me by telling me it was much easier. So I signed up, and then my friend suggested I try out for the school paper. I balked and said, "I've never done anything like that. I could never write for a newspaper." But he kept at it and finally I gave in.

The editor sent me down to the other end of town to cover the sophomore basketball team. When the paper came out next week, lo and behold, there was my article. They had chopped about three quarters of it out, but it was still mine! I kept on writing and next year I became assistant sports editor. The year after, I was sports editor. The year after that I was managing editor.

If anybody had said to me when I was a green sophomore,

"By the time you graduate from this school you'll be second in command of the school paper," I'd have told them they were crazy. I wouldn't have believed it, because the voices in my head were saying, "You don't know how to write. You can't do this." If it hadn't been for my friend's persistence, I wouldn't even have tried. And now I've written ten books! So you never know until you try.

The same thing happened to me with writing fiction. After I became an author, I used to say to myself, "Dodson, you're good at nonfiction, but you don't have any talent for writing fiction." Then six or seven years ago, for some obscure reason, I tried it. And it worked. I'm not as good at fiction as nonfiction, but with my friend and writer Paula Reuben, I wrote a science fiction book for children aged eight to fourteen. If you had asked me ten years ago if I could do that, I'd have said, "Certainly not." And I would have been as wrong about myself as I was when I was fifteen. Or as you might be about some undiscovered parts of your own personality.

If you are on the timid side, it will be hard for you even to get on the phone and create a single parents group. When you are getting ready to do something like this for yourself, always picture it in your mind and picture its successful outcome. For instance, picture a group of eight to ten women gathered in a room, and you participating in the discussion of the group.

Now here's a technique that can help you create a spirit of excitement in your life. Get about twenty 3×5 cards and on each one write an idea for an experiment. Some will be "heavy" ideas, others funny or absurd. Mix the cards up in a shoe box and draw one out every week or twice a week, and do whatever it says. Here are some sample ideas for your surprise box:

> Get on a bus and ride it all the way around your city. Pick out a woman who is a complete stranger and engage her in conversation. Start by asking her directions to some place you already know.

> Next time you are out and run into a woman wearing a particularly attractive piece of clothing—a dress, a blouse, a shirt—compliment her on it. Then get into a conversation about women's clothing. (The things you can talk about

with a perfect stranger are as plentiful as the sands on the beach.)

Conduct a performance of your favorite songs or symphony. In the privacy of your home, turn on the radio, phonograph, or tape recorder and lead the beat. Be aware of the musicians you are directing.

Most grocery store employees wear name tags. For an entire week, when you go marketing, address each employee you talk to by his or her name.

Pick out some interesting-looking person in a meeting or a class and strike up a conversation about the subject of the evening. Then suggest that you and he or she have coffee together.

The main thing is to try out something you have never done before. If you find that it works for you, then you have added a new part of "you" to your personality.

I can guarantee you that if you don't do some of these things, you are never going to discover how large your personality really is. You are never going to discover your full self.

Don't think that the exercises are silly. They are very realistic in a way, and they will help you to do something different. When you have the all-alone blues, one of these is a very good antidote.

I'm not promising any "instant miracles." You are not going to go to sleep feeling sexually inhibited and wake up in the morning feeling powerful and sexually uninhibited. But I remember a man who was in group therapy and told the group about his new girl friend. He said, "She told me that before she had therapy she was timid and cold with men." He said, "I know she's telling me the truth, because she tells the truth. But," he said, smacking his hands together, "in my experience with her it's hard to believe that she was ever emotionally inhibited about sex!"

So people can change. You can change yourself, but you must do it one step at a time.

Right now you may be newly single, and you may feel like your life is helter-skelter, a bunch of flotsam with no meaning or form. Your marriage gave structure to your life. But don't long for the old structure. Create a new one. Life is asking you, "What are you going to do?" Are you going to put your life back together in a new, happy, and fuller way by discovering your own inner voice and listening to it? Do it.

20. You: Manager of Your Time

When I was in high school, my studying was pretty much slapdash. But when I got to college I recognized things would have to change. So for the first time in my life, I began to plan my time. I got a big piece of poster board and divided it into days and hours. Then I began to allocate study time to specific spaces on my time board. History was my hardest subject, so I gave it five hours a week. Geology was my easiest, so it had to do with only one hour a week. The rest of the subjects were somewhere in between.

I also figured out a way to study by using the little chinks of time in the week. For instance, I cut 3×5 blank cards into three pieces and put a French word on one side and the English meaning on the flip side. I had a half-hour bus ride to college and a half-hour ride home so I used this time to study my French vocabulary.

I felt that physical exercise was an important thing so I went to the gym and played badminton for an hour each day. Or if no one else was available I played basketball by myself. So that I wouldn't get stale studying, I made a rule: never on Sunday. Also, I decreed that I would not study after 10 P.M. any night.

Now, don't get me wrong. In spite of this strict study schedule, I still had time to be freshman class president, editor of the weekly newspaper, and manager of the debating council. So I left myself plenty of time for extracurricular things.

What was different from my high school study compared to my college study was that in college I had a *plan of study*. It was all written down on my big study calendar. I knew what I had to study and when.

Not that I absolutely followed my plan all of the time. If I felt like phoning a girl, I did it. Or if I felt like taking in a movie, I did it. But the master study plan always kept drawing me back to the world of study.

I think the number of things I had to cope with in managing my time in college was mere child's play compared with what the working mother of today has to cope with in managing her time.

For one thing, she has more unexpected things to cope with than I did. Her child gets sick unexpectedly or the baby-sitter decides to leave for San Diego with no notice.

So it's a hard schedule to maintain. But it can be done if you plan carefully. First of all, get a piece of poster board and organize your time on it.

Next, plan to simplify your life. You want to do as little around the house as possible. Plan one midweek night for yourself. Always have a backup for your baby-sitter. This is vital! In fact, have two backups, one for your baby-sitter and one for your backup!

Now go over the empty spaces on your activity poster and fill them in with what you are probably doing each week. Once you get the swing of things you will be amazed how much more manageable your life seems.

Once you have done these things, you are ready for a Very Important Task. Go over your schedule and commit the ax murder of your activities for the week. Ask yourself, "Do I really need to be doing this? Do I really need to be volunteering for the School Day Association, the Saturday Chowder and Stamp Collectors Association, or any other thing I am cluttering up my life with?" If the answer is "no," strike it out from your activity board.

Once you start wielding your ax, you will be amazed how easy it becomes to knock large holes in your schedule. You may even find yourself cavorting around your schedule board, muttering with glee as you knock holes in your weekly plans. Do not attempt to phone and drop out of activities that night. Give yourself one day's rest so that you will be firm. Then seize your phone. Don't think you are going to get out of the vice-presidency of any of these activities easily. They surely will not accept the simple excuse you do not want to work in their activity anymore. No! No! No! Tell all of them you must take care of your aging mother who has suffered a relapse.

And she is aging faster than anyone thought she would. They may not believe you, but no one will have the guts to challenge this "aging mother" ploy.

Now, where there are holes in your schedule due to the clever work of your ax, *do not put anything in them.* Keep them open. And then as each hole in your schedule comes along, DO WHATEVER YOU WANT TO DO THAT AFTERNOON OR NIGHT. If you want to do something with the children in that time—that is, if you *really* want to do it—do it. But if you don't want to do anything with your children or anyone else in that time, DON'T DO IT. Do whatever it is you want to do. And find activities you really want to be involved in.

Now, without a doubt, the main difference between my schedule as a student and your schedule as a single mother is CHILDREN, CHILDREN, CHILDREN! Here is the way I suggest you handle this most terrible obstacle in your life. First, read up on the family council. (See pages 46–48.)

Next, get a planner and organizer. You can find these at any good stationery store. The planner/organizer usually has a monthly calendar in which you can plan up to a year ahead and a day and week planner. You can use the schedule board you have made yourself, or you can use this part of the organizer. A section for projects. An idea bank. In this section you will put down notes for meetings, thoughts for the day, and creative ideas that pop into your mind. People. In this section you keep information on important people in your life. Finances. This covers every financial aspect of your life. Remind yourself system. Instead of using scraps of paper which always get lost, you write your notes in one place.

There are a number of these organizers on the market. I personally find the Harper House organizer to be the most effective. You can find it in a stationery store or write to Harper House, 3562 Eastham Drive, Culver City, CA 90230, and ask them what local supplier you can get this organizer from. It's expensive but worth its weight in gold.

Let me remind you of something you already know. There are 24 hours in a day, 168 hours in a week, 8736 in a year. They are very impersonal, these hours. If you have messed up your whole life on Tuesday, you will still be served 24 new hours on Wednesday. You have the choice of screwing them up or doing something useful with them. The choice is yours.

It will do you absolutely no good and it will not improve your life or happiness in any way to merely read this chapter. You will have to put this chapter to work in your life. Of course you know that, but I'm just saying it as a gentle reminder. You need to take the suggestions in this chapter and build them into your life every day and every week. Then you are going to find a tremendous difference in your life. I hope you do just that. Good luck.

Incidentally, if you do come up with a new idea or a creative suggestion that has made your life more efficient and happier, please drop me a note in care of my publisher, Harper & Row, 10 East 53rd Street, New York, NY 10022.

21. *Your Major Enemy: Guilt*

This chapter speaks primarily to the divorced single parent. However, if you are widowed rather than divorced, some of the ideas in this chapter just may apply to you, so read it and take what you need from it.

You will be doing many things as a divorced single parent: raising your children, developing outside activities for yourself, making new friends who are probably single parents like yourself, relating to relatives on both sides of your family, dating men and perhaps looking for that special man with whom you might form a new family someday.

But there is one emotional enemy who will be getting in your way of doing a happy and satisfactory job in all these things. This emotional enemy is GUILT.

The guilt can come from many sources. You may feel guilty for getting the divorce. You may also feel it has done terrible things to your children. Often such guilt feelings are irrational. In fact, you may have had a dreadful marriage and a husband who took little interest in the children. But such truths seldom stand in the way of guilty feelings.

These feelings may go back much earlier than the divorce. You may have been taught by your parents to feel guilty when you were only a child. For example, one of my patients remembered a scene when she was nine or ten years old in which her mother was crying and saying to her and her brother, "I work so hard for you children and you don't appreciate me at all!" Both of the children burst into tears and said, "Yes, we do appreciate you, Mother, we do!" You can easily see how a child brought up by a martyr mother like this is going to be full of guilt. But the important thing is not how you got these feelings. The important thing is how your guilt interferes with your life and your parenting in a thousand ways.

In talking about guilt, we usually think of it as that feeling we all recognize. This is *conscious guilt.* It's the kind a person means when he says, "The hotel made a $75 mistake on my bill and I didn't say anything about it and I feel guilty." The person is aware of his feelings. But there is another more subtle feeling called *unconscious guilt.* The person feels guilty but is not aware of it, not aware of it at all.

Here's an example of unconscious guilt. A patient of mine was a partner in a two-man construction company that hired others to work for them. A job coming up for bid was a terrific one, and they both felt that if they could get this job they could make a healthy profit. My patient worked long and hard preparing the bid. He turned the sealed envelope in on Wednesday. That night he awoke in the middle of the night, covered with sweat. He told me, "I suddenly realized I had bid too low. I knew we would easily get the job on such a low bid, but we couldn't do the work without losing money, lots of money. So I had to refigure the bid and make it higher."

He got dressed and rushed down to his office, where he spent several hours revising the bid. Early the next morning he took the new sealed bid and substituted it for the old one.

When the bids were opened the next day he found that his new figures were far too high. His old first bid would not only have captured the job but made money for his company.

He was dumbfounded. He said to himself, "How could I have done such a stupid thing? I've never done such a dumb thing in my whole life."

That's when he decided to seek therapy to help him find out what caused him to do such a crazy thing. He told me about the incident I have just related and explained how his contracting business worked. Then out of a clear blue sky he said, "Well, at least this boo-boo had nothing to do with my divorce."

He didn't realize that he had just used a negation.

It was Freud who first discovered the existence of negations. A negation is a statement preceded by a negative. For example, a person says, "Not to change the subject," and then changes the subject.

So when Dennis said, "At least this boo-boo had nothing to do with my divorce," the translation was that the stupid bid had a great deal to do with his divorce. So I began asking questions about the divorce, which was still in process. Dennis was the son of a conservative minister, and he had been brought up very strictly. He had been taught that no Christian would ever get a divorce. He was not only taught that as a child, but when he filed for divorce and his mother and father learned about it, they immediately came over to talk with him and pray about it. So Dennis was very guilty about getting a divorce.

The formula for unconscious guilt is as follows: The person is full of guilt but doesn't realize it. He has learned in childhood that after the guilt must come punishment. But he is now a grown man. Who can punish him? No one! So he must arrange to punish himself. And Dennis did this by messing up his bid. That cleared up the mystery of the stupid mistake, and then we began to work on other aspects of his divorce in which he was unconsciously hurting himself.

So that's unconscious guilt. The terrible thing is that it's an enemy that strikes you in the dark. You feel deeply guilty but are not consciously aware of it. This is truly a terrible predicament. If you don't know you're feeling guilty, how can you keep from punishing yourself for your "misdeeds"?

One typical way that unconscious guilt can hurt a person in a divorce is to cause her to be unfair to herself by messing up the property settlement or child visitation.

Linda told her lawyer, "Look, I just want to get out of this marriage. I don't give a damn about the money. I just want to get out."

The lawyer objected, "But Linda, do you realize that the two of you have $26,000 equity in your house? Half of that is legally yours, $13,000. Surely you don't want to throw that away."

"I don't care about the money or the house. Let him have it all. I just want out."

Linda's lawyer realized that he was dealing with an irrational force in her personality. He felt he needed reinforcement in dealing with it, so he got her to make an appointment with me. She told me the same thing she had told him. She didn't care about the money. I started on a new tack, her children. "Linda, do you realize what you may be doing to your children by giving all of your money and possessions to your ex-husband? The children are going to need this money." Her stiff neck and posture then began to weaken.

Finally I got onto the subject of guilt. Yes, she felt guilty, and the feeling was just under the surface. She had wanted to erase the memory, but reluctantly she told me that two years before, when the marriage was particularly bad, she had had an affair. We explored her feelings about the affair. And I was finally able to get her to see that it was guilt that was causing her to give her husband all of the financial assets of the marriage. It was an unconscious attempt to pay him off for having had the affair.

Linda's case is a typical one, and lawyers are often baffled when a person wants to throw her money away. Once the divorce is over, the mother then begins to feel terribly guilty about her children. But that guilt too is usually unconscious. She feels she owes them things to make up for the divorce. This is likely to make her unduly lax with their discipline. If the children are the type who manipulate, she will be putty in their hands. They will know they can always con her into doing what they want. If she starts out the door with a friend and they cry, "Mommy, Mommy, don't leave," that cry will pierce her like a knife. She is supposed to be the parent, but the children are really the parents and Mother is the helpless child. Every time the mother needs to be firm, her load of guilt pulls her down.

Now for the key question: Is there a way for Mother to get rid of this burdensome guilt? Yes, there is. I call the technique The Art of Negative Thinking.

Almost everyone has heard about "positive thinking." If your boss is mean and spiteful, you picture him as friendly and helpful. If life rains on you, you picture the sun shining. But there is one thing wrong with this technique. For most people, it doesn't work. When people find themselves ripped by severe anxiety or depression, positive thinking is like putting a Band-Aid on a spurting artery. Positive thinking is not powerful enough to deal with the deep, unconscious forces of the mind.

Instead of positive thinking, I suggest you use negative thinking. Here's how it works. Many years ago a psychologist named Dr. Knight Dunlap was learning how to type at the age of thirty-five. He found he was making a persistent error, typing "hte" instead of "the." No matter how hard he practiced, he couldn't overcome his bad typing habit. So he decided to try something different. He *deliberately* typed the mistake "hte" about 200 times. When he finally got back to "the" he found he could now type it correctly.

This is why his new method worked. He wanted to type "the" but unconsciously, against his conscious will, "hte" kept coming out. So he took the involuntary and unconscious error and put it under his conscious control.

Using this method, Dr. Dunlap successfully worked with people who were learning to type, play the piano, send Morse code, or perform other mechanical activities. I have extended Dr. Dunlap's concept to the area of feelings and emotions. I teach people to get rid of undesirable feelings and emotions and replace them with healthy and desirable ones.

Let's take the feeling of guilt that is such a plague on single mothers.

We can start with the guilt that Mother feels when she has a date and her little girl yells, "Mommy, Mommy, don't leave me." Now we'll need to rehearse this several times before trying it in real life. What you do is to role play your thoughts, giving voice to the negative tapes in your head, exaggerating them as much as you can.

Imagine the scene where your daughter is screaming, "Don't leave me!" Then say to yourself, "How can you be so cruel to your little girl? She's been devastated by the divorce, which is all your fault. You're such a *terrible* mother. You don't deserve to go out on a date tonight," and so on and on. These are the feelings that have been operating in your conscious or unconscious mind, but *silently*. What makes them so powerful is their silence. When you get them out into the open, they lose some of their power.

When you are airing your negative tapes, don't try to correct or disagree with them, no matter how irrational they are. Just continue to exaggerate all the guilt feelings you have. Sooner or later, if you keep playing the tapes to yourself in exaggerated form, you are going to hear a little voice inside you saying, "That's baloney." And that's the first step toward breaking the hold of your guilt messages. Continue to play the role of the accusing tapes, and they will sooner or later vanish from your mind. Then whenever a new guilt feeling comes into your mind, simply start the role playing all over again.

After a while you may begin to laugh at your former twinges of guilt. When your eight-year-old cries to you, "Mother, don't leave me," you can silently say to yourself, "Not me, I have not ruined that child's life by getting a divorce." Then march out with your date.

Instead of always practicing negative thinking alone, you could teach your emotional support group how to have a hilarious time getting rid of guilt feelings together. A group is particularly fine for doing this. One of you plays the role of the guilt tapes, and the rest of you play the role of the intelligent positive tapes.

This is the single best psychological technique I know to get rid of guilty feelings. Practice as much as you reasonably can, and you will sooner or later notice the guilt fading away. As it does, you will be starting to feel a lot better about yourself, your children, and the divorce. And you will have a new sense of freedom.

22. Creative Selfishness

Unselfishness is as American as Mom, hot dogs, and apple pie. While you are reading this, people all over the country are urging other people to be more unselfish.

Parents are telling children, "Now, Lewis, don't be selfish. Share some of your toys with your brother." Teachers are telling their students to be more unselfish. Wives are saying to husbands, "Don't be so selfish with the TV. The rest of us want to watch something besides football all the time." Husbands are saying to children, "Come on, quit hogging the TV. I want to watch some football instead of those stupid videos." Pastors are telling parishioners, "Selfishness is what ruins marriages and causes dissension among people. Strive to be unselfish."

If you listen carefully to these words you will notice an interesting fact. Selfishness is always something the other guy has that the speaker thinks he should get rid of. That's why I call selfishness the "other guy's disease."

Even though many people feel that selfishness is bad and unselfishness is good, I beg to disagree. I think unselfishness has caused more trouble between people than any other personality trait I can think of. Unselfishness is the cancer of the mind.

Let me give you an example of the bad effects of unselfishness as it concerned one single parent. This mother later became a patient of mine. She was thirty-eight when her husband died. Her daughter was eleven. For the next ten years the woman sold life insurance. She worked a harrowing schedule. She started at nine in the morning and didn't get home until nine or ten at night. She told me, "I was so exhausted when I got home I didn't even feel like watching TV or reading. I just crashed into bed to get ready for the next day."

"But why did you work such an exhausting schedule?" I inquired.

"It was for my daughter. I wanted to have enough money to send her to a good college. My daughter is my life! Do you think I would be selfish enough to neglect my daughter? No, it was all for her!"

Now, here is the really interesting part of this story. After all those years of the mother's sacrifice, the daughter chose not to go to college! The mother was heartbroken. Worse, the daughter had become sexually promiscuous and was going out with a stream of wild boys. That is the point at which the mother began consulting me. We worked hard together to repair all the things that had been caused by the mother's "unselfishness."

You might think that the daughter would appreciate her mother's hard work and all the things she had done without so that the girl could have nice clothes and go to college. But she did not. And this is not an unusual situation. It happens all the time.

What I worked on with the mother was to teach her to be creatively selfish. To have a life of her own. To cut down on her working hours. To start dating (which she had not done for ten years because of her work load). To spend time with her friends. To require her daughter to pay room and board out of the money she earned at work. The daughter objected violently to this until the mother suggested that perhaps the daughter would rather pay for her own apartment and her own food.

All of these changes caused the daughter to begin to respect her mother for the first time. Instead of seeing her as a human slot machine, disgorging goodies when you pressed the right buttons, she now began to see her as an independent person with rights and feelings of her own.

One effect of raising your children "unselfishly" is that they can grow up with the idea that other people should wait on them. They also see that their mother never seems to have time for fun in life. All mother does is work, work, work. Where is the fun for her? Mother is also indirectly teaching them to manipulate people. She is a model of manipulation, because she expects her unselfish behavior to win their love,

good behavior, and sympathy. And she herself is always there
to be manipulated. Her psychological stance is to be ready at
any time for her kids to push her around. Another sad result
of this kind of unselfishness was that one or more of the kids
may try to emulate her. A child who has an "unselfish" mother
often grows up to be the same herself.

Unselfishness sounds like such a wonderful thing. But when
you analyze these examples, you see what's wrong with it. It
isn't really unselfishness at all. It's a reaction to guilt, as we
discussed in the last chapter. Or it's a reaction to fear or to
early modeling by a martyr mother. Or it's a need to be pitied
or loved, or an attempt to control the children. Whatever it
is, it's emotionally unhealthy. Because it pretends to be one
thing while being another, no matter how sincere the parent
may feel. It sacrifices the good of one person for the benefit
of another, with an outcome that is usually unfortunate. This
kind of unselfishness is a rose garden with a snake in it. And
sooner or later somebody is going to be bitten by that snake.

Here's another example. It concerns a student and his parents and uncle at the dinner table. It was Christmas, and in
the Stapleton home Cedric was a high school senior. The talk
drifted toward the financial costs of colleges these days.

"I think I'll be accepted by one of the top places, like Yale
or Harvard or Princeton, but that's not the problem," said
Cedric. "The problem is being able to pay for it. I've applied
for several academic scholarships, and I hope one of them will
come through."

But Blake, his father, said, "Don't go getting your hopes
too high. Remember the old adage 'Don't count your chickens before they're hatched.' "

"Blake," said Uncle Henry, "this time maybe we can cap-
ture some of those chickens before they're hatched. I've given
Cedric's situation a lot of thought. I know it's financially impossible for you to put him through one of those top-rated,
expensive schools. But there's more than one way to skin a
cat. And here's one that will surprise you." Then he turned
to his nephew. "It's a full scholarship, and it can only be won
by a red-headed boy named Cedric, and its donor is none
other than his uncle. I'm not a rich man, but I'm retiring now
and about to collect my pension fund. I might have had other

plans for it, but nothing is more important than the education of my brother's son. As long as you are getting good grades, it will be good until you finish whatever college you pick."

The room exploded with clapping and cheers. Cedric hardly knew how to handle this fantastic piece of news. He was thinking to himself (but didn't say it aloud), *Uncle Henry is the most generous and unselfish man I know. Imagine, giving up his own plans so that I can go to college. And he doesn't want anything in return!*

So Cedric went off to college his freshman year. He found that everything had been paid for: tuition, dormitory, even his books and supplies.

Uncle Henry's birthday was November 21. The family had always reminded Cedric to send a birthday card to him. They knew how much he appreciated such little remembrances. But this year, with Cedric away at college, somehow his folks didn't get around to reminding him to send a card. Cedric completely forgot his uncle's birthday. But he would never forget the uproar that followed when Uncle Henry didn't get that card. Uncle Henry was furious. He called up Cedric's parents and chewed them out for Cedric's omission. "Look at this situation, just look at it. I spend $15,000 for Cedric to go to a really fine college. And how does he thank me? He can't even go to the trouble of sending me a card on my birthday. It's disgraceful. That's the last money he's going to get from me!"

So there were strings attached to Uncle Henry's so-called generosity and unselfishness after all. Cedric found out the hard way.

Unfortunately, the structure of the single family is a setup for that snake in the rose garden, unselfishness. The single mother is all alone and has few people to help her out with all the work she must do. So it is easy for her to cast herself in the role of victim.

A family I knew contained an eighteen-year-old who was adept at getting her way with her mother. When her mother remarried and the new couple planned a trip to Hawaii, the girl decided she'd like to go along. The new husband objected, but his wife said, "You wouldn't want Samantha to be left out of something so precious as our honeymoon, would you? We mustn't be that selfish." So the husband shut up and Samantha went to Hawaii with them. The trip was a disaster. The marriage had gotten off to a terrible start, and the couple finally came to see me.

I tried to give both husband and wife a chance to air their sour grapes. We were only about ten minutes along when the mother, who didn't like to hear these things or think about them at a deep level, bolted out of the room. She was learning about herself. So she left and never came back. The husband stuck it out for a year and then moved out. The mother's insistence on unselfishness with a manipulating child had cost her a husband.

Don't let your family get bitten by the snake in the rose garden. Don't be unselfish with your children. Instead, have the courage to be selfish in a unique and creative way. And raise your children that way. A creatively selfish child doesn't run over other children, but she doesn't let them run over her either.

I am talking about raising your child with self-esteem. This is simple to talk about but hard to do if you've been raised to be unselfish yourself. And perhaps seen your own mother playing the role of victim when you were growing up.

To raise your children to be creatively selfish and have healthy self-esteem, here is what you need to do:

First, if you are sacrificing yourself for the imagined good of your children, stop that. Be a model of self-esteem yourself. You will find this difficult until you get the hang of it.

The other thing to do is to use the positive reward system to train your children. Whenever one of your children shows behavior that exhibits healthy self-esteem, praise her for it. If she pulls an "unselfish" act, ignore it. Don't berate or chastise her, because even bad attention is a form of reward.

It may take time to help your child form habits that lead to healthy self-esteem if you've been modeling the victim and praising unselfishness for years. The change takes time, but it will eventually happen. And the more your child shifts over to creative selfishness, the easier it will be for you to do the same. After a lifetime of martyrdom, whether great or small, emerging as a woman with true self-esteem is exciting.

If you need encouragement or convincing, here is an example of how creative selfishness can benefit everyone.

A psychology student was wrestling with the decision about whether to stay here in the United States with his elderly mother or go abroad for further study. He decided to go abroad for study leading to his Ph.D. in psychology.

The mother was sixty-two at the time and did not want him to leave her. Eight of her friends wrote and told him not to go. After all, his mother was elderly and might die soon, and then he could leave. When he decided to leave anyway, the writers of the letters condemned him as selfish.

But the mother actually lived until the age of ninety-three. She told her son a few months before she died that one of the best things he had ever done for her was to pursue his studies abroad. She had been sad and angry when he left, but later she realized she was proud of his independence and will to succeed. And his absence had kept her from becoming an old lady dependent on having her child around, as so many of her friends were.

Do nothing for anyone else that is not also good for yourself. This does not mean that you have to profit from it in some material way. You can do something for someone because you really feel rewarded by it and that's your only benefit. But don't cross over the line that divides pleasure from imagined pleasure, where you're sacrificing yourself for someone else and telling yourself it feels good. That's negative and harmful for both of you.

The self-denying mother usually has a number of special psychological traits that go with her so-called unselfishness. For example, she is partly a martyr. She is also (secretly) proud that she is unselfish. She enjoys wringing that last bit of sympathy from her children and friends.

For most of her adult life this mother complains to her children (and repeats it to her friends) that they are wearing her out. The children are supposed to say, "Oh, what a hard job you have, Mommy! It's terrible how hard you have to work. And, oh, Mama, I almost forgot, I'm going to the junior high dance tonight. Could you iron my blue dress for me?" Mother sighs and gets up out of her chair. "You could have let me know earlier, but that's all right, that's the way children are and that's the love of a mother."

This scene is enacted over and over until her last child leaves the nest. And then what can the mother do? She has been doing things for the children until she is blue behind the ears, but now there are no more children to mother, and she is ill prepared to do good things for herself. Too bad.

Many centuries ago, Jesus looked with distaste at the character traits he observed in the Pharisees, who were the chief unselfish people to be found in his world. Jesus pointed out to the Pharisees (and incidentally to the lawyers with them) that they were unselfish on the surface but full of "dead men's bones" inside.

The Pharisees were similar to the unselfish people I have been talking about. Because if you are unselfish you tend to end up like the Pharisees: with a holier-than-thou attitude. You look down your nose at other people. You feel you are a specially good person and that other people who are selfish are not as good as you.

When my son Rusty and I joined the Boy Scouts when he was eleven, everybody except one other boy called me Dr. Dodson. The other boy, Ashley, called me Fitz from the first time he met me. I liked Ashley. I liked his healthy self-assurance. I later met his parents, and I saw that from early childhood they had given their son the freedom to be creatively selfish. And I knew that they had helped him build the foundation for a bright future.

You can do the same thing for your own children and yourself.

23. How to Find a Good Man

Perhaps you are planning on a manless future. Maybe you are going to take vows of celibacy. Or you think that men are the pits and you're not going to clutter up your life with them. If so, read no further. This chapter is not for you.

But if you want to find a good man, as a husband or lover or just a steady relationship, I can tell you how to put him in your life.

It seems rather elementary to point out that for a man and a woman to get together and become involved they first have to meet. Some men and women meet through their work. That's very convenient. But waiting around the office for the right man to materialize can take a long, long time. There are better ways not only to find a good man, but to have a choice among many interesting and eligible men.

In today's relations between the sexes, some women are still guided by the myth that the truly feminine woman should never take the initiative. She must sit helplessly by and wait for a bold, assertive male to notice her and make the first move to meet her. Even if he is shy and stumbling, it's still his official role to approach her, although she may have to guide his faltering footsteps.

Many women have already cast off their barriers to assertiveness in the business world. They have done this for a simple reason. They have learned that nonassertiveness does not pay off and assertiveness does. Although women are beginning to taste the fruits of assertiveness in business, some are only tentatively and hesitantly beginning to be aware that assertiveness also pays off in man-woman relationships. And please do not confuse assertiveness with aggressiveness. *Assertive* merely means standing up for your rights and asserting your needs and wishes in a situation or relationship. *Aggressive* has an adversary connotation to it. *Aggressive* means being pushy and hostile in getting your way.

In this book I am not going to teach you to be pushy or aggressive or hostile. Many women feel that being aggressive takes away from their femininity. But being assertive does not in any way detract from your femininity. It only adds spice to your personality. So I am going to teach you how to be assertive—to take the initiative—with a man you would like to meet in such a delightful way that he will soon become interested in you.

The Four-Step Meet-a-Man Method

Here is a typical scenario that you might find at an art museum any Sunday. You are a single woman, thirty-two years old, and reasonably attractive. You have come to the museum to see a new exhibit of Picasso prints. As you stroll through the exhibit, you notice someone else in the museum. This someone else is an interesting-looking man. You say to yourself, "Now there's somebody I'd like to meet." But there is usually a sad ending to this little story, because he does not come over and start a conversation with you. He simply continues walking through the museum looking at the Picassos and so do you. Finally, he leaves the museum and so do you. But not together. The title of this scenario is "The Relationship That Never Got Started." Why didn't it get started? Because you were inhibited by the old myth that the man must make the first move.

Now let's see how this scenario could have worked out if the woman knew how to handle it. Here is the Four-Step Meet-a-Man Method.

You are standing gazing at a Picasso print when you notice at the other end of the room a very interesting-looking man who appears to be in his middle thirties. You say to yourself, "Now there's a nifty-looking guy. I wonder if his brains match his looks? I think I'll go over and find out."

So you wander over to where he is standing and put into action the four-step plan. First you approach him and say, "Pardon me, may I tell you something?"

He looks a little startled but replies, "Why sure, I guess."

He will always give you permission to say something to him, to satisfy his curiosity if nothing else. You have taken the first step. Now you move on to step two. You say in your own words something like, "I think you're a very attractive man."

"Well, thanks," he says, "you've made my day."

Now you're ready for step three. You tell him, again in your own words, "As I was standing over there and you were standing here I said to myself, 'If I just let nature take its course, you will go your way and I will go my way and we will never get to meet each other.' So I gathered up my courage and came over to speak to you."

"That's really terrific," he says. "It's not often, to put it mildly, that I get approached in this way by a good-looking woman. By the way, my name's Harry Blake."

"I'm Cathy Winkler," you say. You are now ready for the fourth and final step.

"Look, Harry, we could stand here and hold up the walls of this art museum for some time. But I think it would be fun to go somewhere and get a cup of coffee or a drink."

"Sounds like a good idea."

Harry is not aware of it, but when he says yes to your invitation to coffee or a drink he has really agreed to talk with you for about twenty minutes. When you first saw him, all you were attracted to was his looks. You had no idea what kind of character or personality he had or whether he had any brains. Now you are in the fortunate position of having at least twenty minutes to find out the answers to these questions.

It's important for you to practice the Four-Step Meet-a-Man Method before using it. Find the words that feel right to you, and practice till it sounds natural, not like a tape recording. In order to be successful at it you must feel comfortable with your approach.

This is such a wonderful method for meeting men you will wonder why more women don't use it. The reason is simple: FEAR. They are afraid of rejection. But once a woman has used the four-step method successfully several times she will feel reassured that in no way is she going to get rejected.

Realistically, you must be prepared to get rejected once in a while. But think what men have been going through for years getting rejected by women. I have a friend who says if you're not getting rejected at least once a week you're not trying hard enough to meet somebody new.

The beauty of this method is that you can use it literally anywhere as a way of meeting a man. In a supermarket, a health club, an airport, a hotel lobby, an art museum, a theater, even walking along the street. That last one is harder, but it can still be done.

It's wonderful to have a man friend you can call to bail you out of a lonely, sit-at-home evening. Or who's available when you need someone to talk to or an escort for the theater or a party. Someday you will marry again, when you find the one man you want to spend the rest of your life with. But in the meantime, you will have built yourself a wonderful circle of interesting and attractive male companions.

Perhaps you are thinking, "I could never go up to a strange man and introduce myself; my personality just isn't built that way." My response to this is simple. Continue to sit home in your apartment and watch TV while other women are out meeting the men.

Singles Places

One of the advantages of the four-step plan is that it is a one-on-one situation. You are not competing with any other woman in any way. It is the absolute opposite of the singles bar, singles dance, or singles group. There you are at a great disadvantage unless you happen to possess a stunning face and figure. And if you are this great looking, then you don't have to worry about the competition.

Some methods of meeting men are good for some women and other methods are better for other women. You have to find the way that's best for you. If you are really turned on to singles events, then by all means go to them. But give the four-step plan a try too.

It Pays to Advertise

Advertising is a much misunderstood and underrated method of meeting some great men. It's a highly effective, if unconventional, technique. Many women are concerned that if they place an ad in a singles magazine or newspaper, they will meet a lot of weirdos and creeps. These fearful fantasies, however, bear little resemblance to the high quality of men you can meet by answering ads in a singles magazine or paper like the *National Singles Register*. Many divorced and widowed people, both male and female, have been very successful in meeting compatible singles through these magazines and newspapers. For example, a widow I know met a professor of philosophy at UCLA, whom she later married.

Let's take a look at the kind of ad we're talking about:

> Attractive college graduate, 38, 6'2", sensitive, romantic, enjoys hiking, camping, the beaches, music of all sorts, dancing and dining out, tennis, browsing in bookstores or libraries or museums. Seeks woman to 35.

This ad will have a code number such as H301. If the ad intrigues you and you want to meet the man behind the ad, you simply write him a letter.

Now let's talk about the letter you write. It is as important as the letter you might send with a job résumé in applying for a position. But many women foolishly dash off a few scrungy lines on a bit of scrungy paper that looks as if it had been rescued from the cat box. Then magically they expect to make a favorable impression on the man who reads it. Here is an example of what I mean:

> *Dear H301:*
>
> *Read your ad and would like to hear from you. From reading your ad I thought I would like to meet you. I am 45, from New York, have been divorced three years, and have three teenagers. I do not have a recent photo at this time. I live at 1601 South Atchison, San Diego 22643.*

This letter is really bad. The writer does absolutely nothing to describe herself as an interesting and desirable woman. She seems to think that by merely stating that she wants to meet the ad writer, he will immediately become motivated to meet her. Although he has said that he is thirty-eight and wants to meet women up to thirty-five, she completely ignores this and acts as if he hadn't said it. She tells nothing of her

likes and dislikes or her uniqueness as a person. In short, she
tells nothing that paints a positive picture of herself so that
he would want to meet her. If we can assume that she is
reasonably good looking, she does not even go to the trouble
of getting a good photo to send as a means of getting him
interested. The odds are something like a million to one that
shortly after opening her letter he will place it gently in his
round file.

Let's contrast that dismal letter with a good one. This is an
actual letter, changed a bit to protect the identity of the writer.
And for the sake of brevity I'm not using the whole letter. But
it is obvious that this woman has devoted a great deal of
thought to her letter. It is carefully and warmly written.

> *Dear H301:*
>
> *I loved your ad. It reads of quality and education, which are
> two of the things I'm looking for in a man. You sound delight-
> ful and I would truly enjoy meeting you. I am intelligent and
> a graduate of the University of Michigan. I love good books
> as evidenced by my bookshelves. When they turn me loose in a
> bookstore or library I usually come home with an armful. I'm
> blonde, 5'5", 35 years old, and am told I'm very attractive.
> I like hiking, jogging, and the outdoors. I love to go out to
> dinner and dancing and I enjoy gardening and grow a lot of
> my own vegetables. I'm looking for someone who is gentle,
> masculine, and compassionate. I enjoy going to nice places as
> much as anyone but first and foremost I desire and maintain
> a solid home life. You may be swamped with replies to your ad
> but I hope you will recognize quality and put me at the top of
> your list to meet. My phone number in the evenings is 936-
> 8240. You can also reach me at work during the day at
> 813-4545. I hope you like my photo but it's not anywhere near
> as neat as the full three-dimensional woman! Please give me a
> call.*

Notice the difference between these two letters. The second
woman tells a great deal about herself as a person. I feel the
man would certainly say to himself, "Say, that sounds like an
interesting person, I want to meet her." And he would pick
up the phone to call. By the way, did you notice that the first

woman did not even give a phone number? The second one gives not only her home phone but also her office phone, so that he can reach her more easily.

Everything you do to make it easier for the man to respond to your letter is to the good. Notice also that the woman is not afraid to be assertive. She suggests that no matter how many replies he has gotten to his ad, he will recognize her quality and put her letter up to the top to be answered early.

Now I want to talk about how to write an ad. First let's discuss how *not* to write one.

> I'm a hardworking, fun-loving woman with a zest for life. I refuse to get in a rut. I love people and parties but still like the quiet of my own home. I'm an attractive, compatible, and compassionate person. 42, 5'3", blond hair. I'm from the Midwest originally.

If you examine this ad closely, you will see that it tells too little about the writer. You get no feeling for her individual personality. For example, she lets you know that she enjoys parties but also enjoys the quiet of home. Who doesn't? There's nothing distinctive in that. She also wastes a whole sentence by informing her readers that she's from the Midwest, as if they cared. She also uses the word *attractive* to describe herself. When you read the ads, you will see that about 99 percent of the women use that same word. Apparently there are no unattractive women advertising in the singles newspapers or magazines! Be imaginative! Come up with some other way to describe yourself other than that weary, worn-out word *attractive*.

Here's an example of an ad I think does the job. Note that it begins with what professional writers call a hook; that is, the opening sentence hooks the reader's interest. Furthermore, notice that by the time you finish reading the ad you have a fairly good idea of the unique woman who wrote it. Incidentally, it is almost impossible to write a short, inexpensive ad that will still be intriguing. To write a good ad you're going to have to write a fairly long one, which will cost you money. If you're not prepared to invest a little money in a good ad, then forget it.

Here's what I call a very good ad:

I'm looking for a man who probably doesn't exist. He's intelligent, tall, reasonably good looking, warm, open, and genuine in his feelings, fun loving, with a healthy sense of humor. He likes music from classical to jazz, dancing and dining out, reading and browsing in bookstores, libraries, and museums. Movies and the theater, tennis and hiking, spectator sports such as football and basketball.

What do I have to offer such a special man? Well, 823 past boyfriends, when interviewed by the *Singles Register,* rated me as "great looking." 314 rated me "the pits." But what do they know? I possess all of the same characteristics that my special man has, and one that he probably doesn't: I am a good cook and I like cooking. I'm 42, a redhead, 5'5", slender. I am a unique woman and I want to meet a unique man.

The responses you will get to your ad will typically fall into three categories. One extreme will be the klutzes and klucks. You will have no trouble spotting them from their letters. For example, one man answered an ad with two single-spaced Xeroxed pages in which he described much more about himself than anyone but his mother would be interested in. Believe it or not, he had several quotations from his Sunday school teachers telling what a wonderful person he was! He also had an unverified quotation from his army sergeant, saying what a fabulous private he had been during boot camp. He attested to his willpower by enclosing a graph showing the number of pounds he had lost over the past two years. The letters from the klutzes will each be quite different, but you will have no trouble in knowing that you do not want to meet them.

On the other extreme will be the letters you immediately recognize as having been written by delightful people. These are the ones you will begin answering.

In the middle of the spectrum will be a group of letters that are neither delightful nor klutzy. Don't ignore these letters. Very few adults in our society can write decently, and therefore very few adults write decent letters. But these people may turn out to be very nice when you meet them, even though their letters don't thrill you.

When it comes to making a date, be sure not to make it any earlier than a week away. As for where to meet, you have two basic choices: your apartment or house or neutral turf such as a restaurant or hotel for the first date. If he turns out to be an obnoxious person who is hassling you or he's incredibly boring, it's much easier to get away from him on neutral ground. Also a neutral place is safer.

Here is an excellent singles publication in which you can advertise: the *National Singles Register.* The address is P. O. Box 567, Norwalk, CA 90650. Even though this newspaper is based in southern California you can use it to place and answer ads regardless of where you live.

Other Singles Events

There are many singles groups, which vary according to area. Parents Without Partners is a nationwide organization. It offers events in which both you and your children can participate. It's a good place to size up a man in terms of how he relates to your children and to children in general.

The Sierra Club has a singles section for people who are interested in hiking and camping and nature. Actually, there are many different specialized singles clubs throughout the country. And you may find these very helpful in finding men.

Church groups, evening classes, and other special-interest gatherings—square dancing, photography, wine tasting, politics—are not limited to singles but can be a great way to meet men who are interested in some of the same things you are. Just be sure that in any group you join there are at least as many men as there are women. Having common interests makes it easy to strike up a conversation. But if you have trouble meeting anyone in particular, use the four-step method.

When you are talking to a man at one of these events, imagine that you are hiring him for an executive position in a company. Use questions to draw him out and size him up. What are his hobbies? How does he regard his friends, his family, and other relationships? Ask yourself, is he attentive to you? Is he interesting? What kind of remarks does he make about women? If he comes off flip, demeaning, or sarcastic about women, look out. This kind of sexist attitude has no place in a good intimate relationship.

Remember too to use your intuition in sizing up a man. Intuition is a kind of hunch or feeling, not necessarily bedrock truth. But you can find out a lot of good general information just by paying attention to the subtle vibes you pick up.

Don't overlook the fact that there are probably some very nice, eligible men in your everyday life. Maybe you don't know them yet, but they're there. I've heard many stories about chance meetings that have turned into something special.

It's important to allow yourself the benefit of meeting a variety of men. It helps give you a good basis on which to make a decision about the right man for you. Stop and look at the people at the football game, in the department store, in the shopping mall. Life can turn into a fascinating detective story if you decide to start looking for interesting and loving people and expect to find them.

As a final suggestion, be sure to let your friends know that you are interested in meeting new men. People may assume that you're perfectly content with your lot unless you let them know there's still something you're looking for. Many a beautiful woman has languished alone by her fireside, night after night, because everyone assumed her dance card was already full. Even your women friends may have men acquaintances in whom they're not interested, but who might interest you a great deal.

Well, now you have some assertive, interesting, and productive ways of meeting men. My personal feeling is that advertising in a singles publication is one of the very best ways. Still, an amazing thing can happen when you least expect it. One day a man suddenly pops out of an elevator, bumps into you, and half knocks you down, and the next thing you know you're talking to him and he's taking you out to lunch that day. And suddenly you realize that this could be the start of Something Big.

Intrigue Him on the Phone

All right, let's get down to business. You've met him and he's asked you for a date. How do you handle it?

I suggest you make the date roughly a week away. You may have unlimited time in that week, but if you give him a date too early he may assume you are not very much in demand. What's much more important is that you need a week's time to build up his anticipation.

What does a woman typically do to generate a man's excitement about a coming date? Usually nothing. She may plan carefully to be at her most attractive for the date, but she does nothing to build his eagerness about it. In other words, she doesn't send him messages that are teasers. In the entertainment world a teaser is something put out to the audience to tease them into becoming more interested in the main attraction. TV shows, for example, do not simply wait until Thursday to show their special filming of wildlife in America. Instead they will put out a one-minute teaser Monday through Wednesday telling about the fascinating program on wildlife coming up on Thursday. I suggest you do the same.

Your main aid in building him up for the date will be the telephone. Using the phone for this purpose is largely an undeveloped art. Here is how it's done:

Don't wait for him to call you during the week before the date, because he probably won't. Call him instead. But check out in advance whether he feels comfortable about your calling. Even if he's given you his business card with the number on it, you can't take it for granted that he'll welcome your call. He may still feel it's his responsibility to take the initiative. Simply ask him, "Does this mean I can call you, or do you prefer to call me?" Some men aren't able to be open enough to want the woman to call them. But assuming this man says, "Sure, that's great," the way is clear.

For this kind of phoning, it's far better to call him at home than at work, since you want him to be relaxed and feel like talking. Remember, don't call him at work at all unless he's indicated that it's OK. When you call, be sure to ask whether he's busy before you launch into the conversation. Otherwise you may find him not only preoccupied with something else but annoyed at you. And this isn't exactly what you're trying to achieve.

In this first conversation, whether he has initiated it or you have, your approach could be something like, "Why don't we get acquainted a little bit over the phone if that's all right with you?" Then, "You can tell me a little bit about you and I'll tell you a little bit about me. I'll go first if that would make you feel more comfortable." If he says go ahead, you go first. That gives you a chance to set the mood of the telephone interaction. If he decides to go first that shows he is a self-confident person.

When you're describing yourself, don't rely on what comes to your mind spontaneously. Very few people are good at sounding interesting on the spur of the moment. Instead, plan your telephone call a little. That's important not just the first time you telephone but any time.

Know in general what you're going to say, and try to put in some interesting items that are funny and offbeat. Such as, "I grew up in the jungles of South America, barefoot and pig-tailed." If you don't feel comfortable joking in this way, then by all means don't try. The important thing is to be yourself. But if you think that making some funny comments suits your personality, give it a try. Many men will find such an offbeat approach intriguing.

What you really are doing with the phone call is interviewing him the way a journalist interviews an important person. You want to learn as much as you can about him. One important thing to ask about are his hobbies. Ask, "What kinds of things do you like to do when you're not working?" Lots of people are much more interested in their hobbies than their work. Probably all you have to do to get him talking is ask him about his hobbies. Also, ask him how he got started in his work. People usually like to talk about this.

Compliment him when it's honest. Don't say, "I'll bet you're really good looking," if you haven't met him yet and don't know what he looks like. But you can say such things as, "It's wonderful to hear how fast you've moved ahead in your business." Or "You have a terrific vocabulary." Or "You've got a really great analytical mind. I'll bet that has helped you a lot to become successful." Very few people remember to compliment other people. If you compliment him, you are likely to stand out in his mind as an unusual person.

Of course you will want to be at your conversational best on the phone. There are two ways to become a good conversationalist, the hard way and the easy way. The time-consuming and expensive hard way is to have traveled all over the world and done everything and be able to talk interestingly about anything. Such people are truly fascinating conversationalists. But it's hard to become such a person. So why don't you use the easy way?

I'll tell you the experience of a friend of mine, to illustrate the easy way. A physician I know named Dr. Broxton was at a party some time ago. He met two young men there who had spent a year in oil exploration camps in South America. He had been all through Mexico but had never been in South America, and he was quite interested in it. He asked these men a lot of questions about life in the oil towns. What were the people like? What did they do in their fiestas? And so forth. Most of the conversation was about them and their life in the oil towns. Very little of the conversation was about Dr. Broxton. He asked them questions that he was sincerely interested in and listened intently to their answers. About two weeks after the party he heard by the grapevine that the two young men had said about him, "You know that Dr. Broxton, he's a fascinating conversationalist!"

What made him such a terrific conversationalist? That he talked a lot in a fascinating manner? Not at all. It was that he asked questions and really listened to the answers. And that's how you too can become a fascinating conversationalist!

Most single men, like most single women, feel lonely a certain amount of the time. They wish they had someone to talk to who would genuinely listen to them. But they don't. So what happens when a man goes out on a date? Does the woman gratify his need by asking him questions and letting him talk? Often she does not. Often she takes over and dominates the conversation. This he needs like a hole in the head.

What he needs is a chance to talk and be listened to. You can meet that need and you can start on the telephone. But don't let him endlessly dominate the conversation while you doze at the other end of the line. After he has his chance to do some talking, you can gradually get the conversation onto more of a give-and-take basis. After all, *you* have a need to talk also!

The number of calls you make to him this first week will depend on how receptive he seems. Be sure to have a purpose in mind when you call, and stick to it. Let your instincts tell you what is appropriate as far as subjects or reasons to call. You should be able to gauge his receptiveness by what he says to you and his voice tone. Don't telephone so much that he feels overwhelmed. Remember that your calls to him are only teasers. They are not the main attraction, which is you and the date. With some men, one phone call that first week would be plenty. Another man might delight in calling you back and forth every day before the date.

Don't think your use of the phone with a man has to be confined to the week before your first date. The telephone is one of your most precious assets throughout the relationship. As you use the phone more and more, you will improve in the ease with which you can use it as an extension of yourself. There is hardly a purpose which you cannot accomplish with the phone.

Some people are a lot more outgoing than others and have more self-confidence in talking, whether in person or on the phone. If you're not one of these easy talkers, I'm not saying you have to force yourself to use the phone. But the more you practice with it, the more skill and ease you will gain.

Your main use of the phone is just to let a man know you are interested in him—to compliment him, to find out more about him, to gradually become more and more important in his thoughts.

24. Men, Dating, Sex, and Marriage

We've mentioned chapters which tend to get left out of books on single parenting. Well, this is THE chapter that gets left out. If you read some single parent books you would think that after Mother and Father separate, they each buckle on their chastity belts and don't take them off until it's time for each of them to remarry.

Of course, as all you single parents out there know, this is not true. But the unfortunate Catch-22 is that in your deep unconscious mind you may believe it to be true.

And so you find yourself, Helen, age thirty-four, divorced, after a twelve-year marriage, with two boys six and eight. And you, Gwen, a widow at forty-three, after a happy marriage of twenty-three years, terminated by your husband's completely unexpected heart attack, leaving you with a boy eighteen and a girl thirteen. Both of you women happen to be intelligent, with outgoing personalities. Both of you also happen to have very good figures. It will not take long for men to cluster around and start dating you. And that brings up for both of you the very basic question "What am I going to do about sex?"

You will certainly have no problem finding guides to help you answer this question. One group of guides will offer you rules from the right wing. They will tell you in no uncertain terms, "You must not do anything about sex until after you are remarried. Some passionate kissing is as far as you should let yourself go. That's the rule for a decent woman. Oh, men will be after you all right. That's the beastly nature of men. But it's your duty as a decent woman, a guide for your children, to tell them, 'No!' and mean it. Is a few minutes pleasure worth a lifetime of sorrow?"

Such are the voices you will hear from the rules of the right.

But then there are the voices you will hear trying to entice you with the rules on the left. "Good Lord, Gwen, don't listen to those outmoded mid-Victorian morals. They are ridiculous. Nobody lives that way in our time. Have sex every time you get a chance—and enjoy it! That's the way the women of today live—and why shouldn't you?"

So there you are, Helen and Gwen. Which voices should you heed, the rules on the right or the rules on the left?

I think the rules of the right and the rules of the left are equally stupid. *Because they are rules.* And rules never fit individual cases. Helen and Gwen and Marjorie and Sandy and Mary and Heather are all individual, unique persons. They have come from different individual family backgrounds and any general rules on sex cannot possibly fit all of these different women.

If Helen is deeply in love with Harry and has a deep and strong relationship with him and ultimately wants to marry him, is she going to be content to wait two years until they are married before she has sex with him? So you see, she doesn't fit the rules on the right.

And if Gwen has just started going out with a new man, Jim, and this is their second date, she may be very attracted to him physically. One part of her wants to have relations with him, but another part of her is terribly scared. She has never had sex with a man on her second date and she is scared spitless to do it. So the voices from the left say to her, "Go ahead and do it, Gwen—this is a modern age." These voices only increase her fear. Regardless of what the voices say, she is going to have to wait till she is ready. If she plunges in and has sex before she's ready, she's going to feel terribly guilty.

So now we come to my answer to the problem of sex and the single parent. I don't think you should govern yourself by any rules. You are an individual, so no rule is going to fit you or help guide your conduct.

Instead of rules, listen to those wonderful guides already inside you—your feelings! Your feelings are always going to be based on the totality of your being, including your early childhood upbringing. Your feelings always fit you. And your feelings are always up-to-date.

So if your feelings say, "Kiss that man!" do it. And if your feelings say, "Don't kiss that man!" then don't do it.

To use your feelings as your guide rather than rules that don't fit you cuts across all the questions that women ask themselves or that they debate with other women when they are together.

For instance, should a woman go to bed with a man on the first date? Some say no (that's a rule of the right). Some say why not? (that's a rule of the left). But I say, "What do your feelings tell you?" Listen to your feelings and they will tell you whether to go to bed with him or not.

But you may find that your feelings are mixed. Part of them want you to go to bed with him and part of them do not. In such a case where you have mixed feelings I advise you not do to it. Wait until your feelings are at least 90 percent favorable before deciding to do it.

Here's another question many women ask themselves. "Should I let a man sleep over? Will that have a bad effect on my children?"

To give either a flat "yes" or "no" answer to that would be to lay down a rule. And we have seen how unsatisfactory rules are.

So instead you take your own feeling pulse about whether it's OK for Martin to sleep over. You know your own kids. You know what kind of relationship Martin has with them. So put all of these feelings into your own personal computer and come up with the answer.

By now you notice I'm not telling you you should or should not engage in any particular kind of sexual activity. Because if I did that I would be giving you a rule and what do we know about rules? Rules are bad for you!

When I was giving a lecture once on single parenting a young woman stood up and said, "You seem to be giving us a very revolutionary way of answering sex questions. But who are you to tell us what is right and what is wrong in sex standards?"

I answered, "First of all, I'm *NOT* telling you what is right and what is wrong in sex questions. 'Right' and 'wrong' are rules and I am refraining from giving you *any* rules.

"And second, these ideas are not my own. You might be

amazed to learn that they come from Jesus of Nazareth. Jesus once said, 'The Sabbath (and by that he meant not merely the Sabbath rules, but *all* religious and ethical rules) was made for man, not man for the Sabbath.' By this Jesus is saying any ethical or religious rules are created only for the good of man, but man is not meant to be enslaved by them. That's why Jesus deliberately broke the rule about the Sabbath and the Ten Commandments. He said, 'Doing good on the Sabbath is more important than obeying the rule of not doing any work.' And so Jesus taught an entirely new attitude toward life, one which steered clear of rules. He used the principle of love instead of rules as a basis for deciding your actions. I have used your feelings as a way of determining what you love and what is the loving thing to do in any given situation."

If you use your feelings as the guide for your actions you will see that this principle cuts through all the rules and regulations which others seek to foist upon you. And once you become accustomed to this new principle of using your feelings as your guide you will find you have learned the way to true freedom.

One final word. If you are dating and particularly if you have children, various questions will come up from time to time with respect to how you handle many different kinds of sexual matters. One single bit of advice will cover all of these: Tell the truth, but you certainly do not need to divulge the whole truth about intimate and personal sexual matters. But if you always deal in the truth and never mix falsehood with truth, you will be all right. Many times parents will say children are too young to be told the truth about such things (whatever they are)—they couldn't handle it. Wrong. It's the parents who can't handle it.

25. From Single Parents to Stepparents

When single parents marry, the chances are high that they will marry someone with children and become a stepparent. Sometimes the children will be living in the new stepfamily and sometimes they will only be visiting.

At present there are twenty-four million husbands and wives who are stepmothers and stepfathers. One in every three American marriages is a remarriage for one or both partners. Roughly one in every eight children in the United States today is a stepchild. Each year one million children and half a million adults become members of stepfamilies. With the increasing divorce rates, the numbers of stepfamilies are growing all the time.

In my opinion, it is a big job being a parent. It is a bigger job being a single parent. But the BIGGEST JOB of all is being a stepparent. Why is this so?

Part of the reason can be found in an ad in a singles magazine which I mentioned earlier in this book. This is a line from an ad placed by a thirty-eight-year-old man: "Children all right if they are well behaved." All a perceptive woman needs to do is to read that one line and think about its implications to know that to marry a man with views like that would be to voluntarily play Russian roulette with herself. Why?

Look carefully at the wording. "Children all right," not "children welcomed" or "children enjoyed" or even "children OK," but "children all right." This man's acceptance of children is grudging and lukewarm to say the least. Then we read the fine print: "if they are well behaved." If a woman reads the hidden meaning of that correctly she will know the man is really saying, "Children are all right if they behave like adults only in a smaller size. But children must be quiet, walk softly, never yell, or run around excitedly." In short, to quote the old saying, "Children should be seen and not heard." So if a woman with children of any age marries a man with those views, you can be sure trouble is in the offing. For it is obvious that his definition of "well behaved" and her definition of "well behaved" will probably be 180 degrees apart.

This is only one of many things that can cause difficulty in the stepfamily. For in any other marriage only two people are marrying. But in a stepfamily marriage at least one, and perhaps both, of the people is a package deal: a wife with children or a husband with children.

And in the typical stepfamily marriage the two people act as if the children don't count. They love each other and they're going to make each other eternally happy and that's all there is to it. They may have had some natural thoughts of how the life-styles of the two of them are going to fit together. But they have never paused to speculate how the children (perhaps on both sides) are going to fit together. Before they get married they are blissfully unaware of the crosscurrents of jealousy and envy that are going to surge around all of the adults and children of the family. But it only takes them a couple of weeks to find out about jealousy in the family. Oh, they may have experienced jealousy and sibling rivalry in their old intact family. But they soon learn that jealousy in the intact family is minor-league compared to the major-league jealousy in the stepfamily.

The most typical thing I hear from every stepfamily I know or have counseled is something like this: "I just didn't know what I was getting into! I still love Walter, but I never dreamed it would be like this in our stepfamily."

In fact, there are so many hidden land mines in a stepfamily, the best advice I could possibly give you would be to get some professional counseling before you marry and create a stepfamily. And continue with the counseling as long as you need it. You may say, "But we can't afford to get counseling!" And my answer to that is, "You can't afford *not* to get counseling if you want this family to be like the dreams you have for it."

Don't get me wrong. I'm not saying you can't have a stepfamily which is happy. You can. But you've got to work at it and you've got to defuse a lot of land mines in order to be successful. It isn't easy. But it isn't impossible either. I know some stepfamilies that are at least as happy as some intact families I know. And some of them are happier. The problem is that so many stepfamilies assume that parenting and step-parenting are the same. But they are not the same. For a mother to parent a child whom she has carried in her body and brought to birth and nursed is not the same as to parent a child who has not established those biological bonds with her.

Biological parents have infinitely more time to adapt to being a parent as their children grow up from babyhood. Stepparents all have to go through what I call "instant parent-hood." Like on Tuesday they are not the parent of anybody. But by Wednesday they are the parent of an eight-year-old and an eleven-year-old. Almost all stepparents say the same thing. "I didn't know things were going to be so difficult. Believe me, I didn't!"

Why are people so unprepared for the trouble they encounter in managing children in a stepfamily? Most people do not realize what a bewildering and frustrating set of emotional conditions a stepfamily consists of until they are actually in it. It is like a woman who steps into quicksand. At first she doesn't realize how difficult a situation it is. But when she tries to get out she suddenly becomes aware that she is really in a dangerous place. And it will take all of the strength and knowledge she has to get out.

The stepfamily is shot through and through with jealousy. She has experienced the normal jealousy of children and adolescents in the biological family but that is nothing compared to the jealousy of the new and baffling stepfamily. Never have the members of the stepfamily experienced the poison and the depth of the intense feelings they are feeling toward one another. Not only jealousy but ambivalent feelings are felt constantly in the blended family. When the members of the stepfamily become aware of how ambivalent they feel they are shocked.

Stepparents need to learn to accept and live with those ambivalent feelings. To enter the world of reality of your stepfamily you have to quit kidding yourself and become aware that you have very mixed feelings toward your stepchildren. You are never going to feel the same about your stepchildren as you do about your own children.

So stepparents need to learn to live and tolerate the idealization of the natural parent. For instance, ten-year-old George has a father who comes to visit very little and is an alcoholic. George whitewashes the dark spots in his father's psyche and tells people what a wonderful father he is.

So far I'm speaking as if you only had to contend with jealousy and envy *within* the stepfamily itself of wife and husband and assorted children. I'm speaking as if the other mother and father in the picture (remember them?) were leaving you alone and not hassling you. But unfortunately for you that may be exactly what they're doing. So just when you thought you had things settled down in the stepfamily, you look up and there are a man and a woman with rifles shooting at you! Some of you may think that I'm exaggerating wildly as I write about the potential troubles the stepfamily may have to contend with. If you think I exaggerate just ask any stepfamily you know and can trust to level with you.

You will discover that you are subject to constant heavy barrages of flak by an ex-spouse against one or both of the parents, using the children as pawns. Or the stress could be like the drop, drop, drop of Chinese water torture by the ex-spouse filtered through the children.

The roles of the biological mother and father are pretty clearly defined but the roles of the stepparents are fuzzy and undefined. You are not the parent your stepchild thinks he has and you can never take the place of that parent in the child's mind. So what are you? Simply someone who lives in the same house with your stepchild? It is very difficult to define what you are to this stepchild. You must carve your own role in the family complex. We will go into more detail of how to do this later on.

Stepparents feel that if they found instant love with each other, then the children should find instant love also. But then they realize that was a silly and foolish belief.

What can you do to help ensure that your stepchildren will make the transition into your family with the least difficulty?

First, expect trouble. If you do you will be different from

99 percent of the people who get married into a stepfamily situation. Ninety-nine percent of them enter marriage as happy as clams, little aware of the churning rapids that lie around the bend of the river. All the other people will be dewy-eyed and supremely happy. They have found their soulmate in their spouse. They are really hardly aware of the existence of the children. They are so wrapped up in each other. But very quickly the blinders will be taken off their eyes. At this point the Big Crunch sets in. And they will start saying to their friends, "My Gawd, I didn't know it would be like this! Those kids are ruining our lives!"

Second, things will probably get worse. It will get worse because the stepparents don't understand children. And these children are worse than any other kids they have seen. They are not able to tune into the children and fathom what they are about.

Third, before your stepchild moves in, get help as soon as you can from a psychiatrist, psychologist, or social worker. Don't use a minister or doctor unless he has been trained in psychology. You may say, "But I can't afford it." Listen, friend, you may end up paying more in legal fees than all the consulting fees you would have paid.

Fourth, after marriage, if possible, start married life in a new house or apartment. You may think this is minor. I assure you it is not! Who gets what room or what possession is very important.

I remember a stepfamily consisting of an eight-year-old and a ten-year-old. They were going for a vacation in a motor home. The stepmother had packed her two kids' stuff in two large drawers on a side wall of the motor home. Ricky, the ten-year-old, was complaining to the new stepchild. He said to him softly, "This was always my drawer." The father overheard him and whispered to his wife, "It's been his drawer for five years of trips in this old bus. I guess we ought to give him his preference on the drawers." Ricky broke into a wide grin when they gave him back his drawer. So it does make sense to be careful how you give your children living space, even if it's only a drawer in the side of a motor home.

If the child's parent or the child on his own decides to make subtle, or not so subtle, war against you, this is something else. You could really do without the stiletto remarks, the dirty looks, and the violations of the Potsdam Treaty that occur in the kitchen or the refrigerator or the bathroom. It can really get to be wearying after a day or two. Not to mention a week or two.

It will often be the job of the stepparents to create order out of chaos and light out of darkness. Hah! Hah! The stepparent often thinks, "Look what I'm doing for this kid. He should at least show a little gratitude." One stepchild complained to the mother about the way the stepfather was handling him. She told the father about it and he tried to mend his ways. The next day the child complained to his mother that the stepfather did the same thing again. The stepfather went through the roof.

"Look! If Steven has a beef with me, let him tell me. Here he has come to you for two days in a row. No, dammit! I want direct person-to-person communication in this family!"

Fifth, don't rush the child. Don't attempt to establish a relationship with stepchildren overnight. GO SLOW! Give the child time and space or he will move away from you emotionally.

Here is an example (from Ruth Roosevelt and Jeannette Lofas, *Living in Step*, New York: McGraw-Hill, 1976) of stepparents who tried to rush a relationship with an eight-year-old stepson:

"I love you," she said.

"Bullshit," said the boy. "You don't even know me."

If you're cool and low-key, a present is acceptable, but be careful it isn't something the child will take as part of a psychological maneuver to win him over. If you are careful about it, presents for children under eleven usually work out fine. Teenagers are much more tricky. It shouldn't be too big a present or he will feel overwhelmed and pushed by you. Here are some compatible teenage gifts: two tickets to a good rock concert (he or she can take a friend), tickets to a sports event, or perhaps a record of a rock group he or she really likes. Gifts like these are ones that a teenager will appreciate.

Sixth, make liberal use of the feedback technique. This will help you to keep tuned to the child and help keep your own mouth shut. Resist the temptation to lecture or give advice.

Seventh, use the family council twice a week and more frequently if you have more frequent need of it. The family council offers a place of expression for the children's feelings as well as a place to settle issues without having a lot of grown-up direction.

If you are wondering what to have a stepchild call you, I would say first names are the best beginning. This is something a stepchild feels comfortable with. Do not force a stepchild to use Mother or Daddy. If the child chooses to use Mother or Daddy sometime later that is fine, because at that time he can freely choose those terms himself.

Here are some of the factors that mess up the psychological structure of the new parent in the stepmarriage: Divorced parents generally remarry in a shorter period of time than widowed parents, so the child has fewer emotional patterns of family living to give up.

A dead parent is more likely to be idealized and romanticized. The child is likely to turn hostile and regard the stepparent as an intruder. If the parents are divorced the child will usually have an alternative place to retreat to if things get rough for him in his present home. Divorces take place sooner than death. The children involved in divorce tend to be younger, and younger children seem to have less trouble adjusting to the stepparent situation. If you have never been a parent before you may have a tough time adjusting to children in the house because you do not really know what children are like.

The stepparent-to-stepchild adjustment seems to work best with the very young or young adults. The very young are more pliable to a new parent and the young adults have done more living and can relate better to a parent who knows how to handle them. Teenagers are tough to handle because they are rebellious anyway in the "normal" family situation. And when you try to adjust a belligerent teenager to a new stepparent situation, you have trouble in River City.

Should you legally adopt the child if the other parent has moved away or otherwise gotten out of the picture? Yes, if you want to in that situation. But if the other parent is still very much in the picture, then it would be a big psychological mistake to adopt the child. It would do nothing to improve relations between the three of you.

How should you handle the part-time live-in stepchild, the one who comes for a day or a weekend, or part of or all of a vacation period? The main difficulty may be that the stepchild makes a comparison between the family and plays one family against the other.

Set up a regular schedule of visits and stick to it, deviating only when necessary. If there are several children involved, I suggest giving each of the children separate visits and then later have them all together. This way each child can have his own special relationship. Having all the children together creates a special sense of unity as a family.

It's important for you and your spouse to agree on the ground rules that apply to all of the children.

I have tried to give you a realistic view of stepparenting in this chapter. I hope you have not taken it so personally that it depresses you. I want to close with an optimistic note.

I always try to keep up with what professionals in my field are doing. So I enrolled for a class in stepparenting at UCLA. By the second class I noticed something very unusual. All the five couples in the class were holding hands. This really struck me because I've never been in a class where all the students were holding hands. I asked a question about it. "Why do all you people hold hands?" One man answered for the group. He said, "I guess we have been through so much blood, sweat, and tears we are glad we made it. We hold hands out of gratitude, I guess." Here were these five couples who had survived the slings and arrows of outrageous stepparenthood, who had persevered to the utmost when they got flak from other parents or children and are now able to be settled down to a stable and happy stepparenthood and enjoy it. A wonderful example!

I hope that the information I have given you in this chapter will enable you to construct the same type of happy blended family they have built.

26. *The New American Families*

Many people today are wondering what the American family will be like in the future. Magazine articles on such topics as The American Family in the Year 2000 are always read eagerly. Many people are worried that trends such as they see today will change the American family irretrievably for the worse. So it is fitting that I end this book by giving you one man's views on the trends that are shaping the American family now and will shape it in the future. It is extremely difficult to forecast what the family of the future will look like. About the only way we can forecast it is to say that there will be no *one* family of the future; there will be many families. I will now describe these many families.

My first comment is on the incredibly swift pace of changes that the American family is undergoing. There are parts of the world that have hardly changed a bit in the last 100 years. But that is not our story. Our story is one of ever-increasing change. Here are the predictions I am making based on what is going on in society now:

1. There will be increasing numbers of mothers in the work force. If this is true, then many other changes will follow. The economic output of women will change. The battles to give women a fair economic share in their work will continue. More mothers in the working force will inevitably mean more divorces. The fewer mothers in the working force, obviously the lower the divorce rate. The relationship of mothers and children will change. If the mothers are working full-time or part-time, who will raise the children? A day-care center? A relative? A paid caretaker? All of these factors will be influenced by the fact that there will be more mothers in the working force.

2. The roles of both men and women are undergoing enor-

mous change and this will continue. Fifty years ago the role of the mother and the role of the father were very stable. They had not changed for years and years. Now both the men and the women of America are being pulled in different directions by voices from the right and voices from the left. In one way or another, they are wrestling with questions such as these: Should I marry or pursue a career? If I marry should I have children or not? Where should I put most of my energies, toward my career or toward raising children? What psychological traits constitute being masculine or being feminine? If you want to raise a good argument quickly try bringing up one of these questions at your next meeting of any group or at a party.

3. Stepfamilies will be on the increase. One out of every eight children now is a stepchild. The number will increase in the future. The most important fact about the increase of stepfamilies is that it is much harder to raise children successfully in a stepfamily than in a single-parent family or an intact family. Whereas our society now acts as if stepparents did not exist, stepfamilies will increasingly take a more important part in our family structure.

5. The influence of the feminist movement will continue to be felt throughout our society. Many people underestimate the influence of this powerful force. The feminist movement does not merely consist of the New York "Petiteamazons" who write books and are frequently heard on talk shows. No, if you talk to even the humblest farm mother in Dubuque, Iowa, you will see that the movement has reached even there. Mothers in Kalispel, Montana, Biloxi, Mississippi, and in remote mountain cabins deep in the branches of the Snake River who do not usually intellectualize about feminism will devoutly tell you they are raising their children to be nonsexist. If you ask them to define nonsexist, you will get an answer such as I did once: "Well, it's raising my child to be halfway between masculine and feminine." So do not underestimate the power of the feminist movement. It will influence mothers, fathers, college students, and young children growing up.

6. Single-parent homes will definitely increase. I have tried in this book to give wise and helpful guidelines to raising children in a single-parent home. Remember not to under-

estimate the enormous difficulty of being a happy and successful single parent. This is particularly true if you are a woman raising a boy rather than a girl. Try to put the advice in this book to work.

7. After going through a divorce, many more women will never marry again. Thirty years ago when a woman got a divorce, she wanted to be careful not to make the unfortunate choice of her first marriage again. So she would be doubly careful in picking a new man for a second marriage. That has pretty much changed. Many women now take the attitude that the first marriage was so awful, they are not going to take the chance of getting married again.

I regard this as a most unfortunate decision. It would be similar to having an accident with the first car you ever owned and then decide you would never drive again. It is true the decision never to drive again would prevent you from having another accident. But at the same time it would considerably hamper your life in Los Angeles, Chicago, or any other major American city.

Personally, I think it a much wiser decision to learn how to make a wise choice in a second marriage than to give up marriage altogether. But who am I to tell these marriage-injured women what to do? I am like the farmer who begged the hurricane to go around his house. "But," he said, "it didn't pay much attention to me."

8. More women will never marry. There are many more women than men of marriageable age in our society.

9. There will be an increase in both male and female homosexuality and more gays will be urged to come out of the closet. In some cities such as San Francisco this situation can be handled rather amicably. In other regions of the country, the situation will not be handled amicably at all.

10. Divorce will increase. In fact, it will increase a lot. My view of why divorce will increase is a very simple one. In times past, there were many walls which held back a couple from divorce. There were the church regulations. There were the mores of society. But above all there was the fact that if a woman wanted to get a divorce, she had no economic ground to stand on. She would not be able to make her own way in life.

One by one all of these walls have gone down. Therefore, marriages today have to stand on their own two feet. And the increase in divorce now shows clearly that the two feet of many marriages are composed of clay.

Someday our society will be wise enough to decide that marriage is too important to be left to chance. We will have obligatory courses on marriage in our high schools and voluntary courses on marriage in our colleges. There is very little evidence that our society is wise enough to do something about preparing people for marriage.

11. There will be increasing freedom and openness of speech in America on sexual matters. This increasing freedom will be fought bitterly by conservative groups. The increasing openness of speech will result in numerous tugs of war between parents and adolescents, open libraries and book burning, and other difficulties reminiscent of the Scopes trial.

12. Children will become increasingly intelligent in the future in spite of all the inadequacies of the public and private schools. Their intelligence will rise enormously compared to the intelligence level of the same child years ago. The main reason for the rising sophistication of children in the future will be the two main "schools" which teach children: TV and the transistor radio.

Of course, there will be a few children who will still like to read but they will be in a definite minority. However, if you follow my guidance in this book you will be able to nudge your child into this minority group of readers.

13. The number of people living together without marriage will steadily increase. This will be looked upon with a jaundiced eye by the older members of our society. Nevertheless, cohabitation will continue to flourish.

14. In spite of all these incredible changes in the family, the basic family structure of many years will continue: a breadwinner father, homemaker mother, and children. These will continue mainly in small towns and rural areas. But the main bulk of people in the big cities will be of the variant forms mentioned above.

The tumultuous changes I have sketched in this chapter will alarm a great many mothers and fathers. But if you are alarmed by some new trend in our society you can see that your children are not influenced by this new trend if you follow the guidance given in this book.

Although it may not seem true to you at certain times in your child's life (e.g., adolescence), you as his parent are still the most influence on him (believe it or not!). Do not listen to people who tell you a child of divorce must turn out unhappy or twisted. There is no scientific evidence for this. If you do a good job of raising him along the lines given in this book, he will turn out to be the good person you intended to raise.

About the Author

Dr. Fitzhugh Dodson is an internationally known child psychologist and the author of ten books on child raising. His bestselling books on parenting *How to Discipline With Love* and *How to Parent* have been translated into thirteen languages and sold over a million copies each. He is also the author of *How to Father, How to Grandparent,* and *I Wish I Had a Computer That Makes Waffles*, the first book of modern nursery rhymes since Mother Goose, and is the coauthor of *The Carnival Kidnap Caper*, a book of science fiction for children. Dr. Dodson is a clinical psychologist in Redondo Beach, California, where he practices individual and group therapy with children, adolescents, and adults, as well as marriage counseling and parent education. He brings over twenty-five years of professional work as both a psychologist and an educator and personal experience as the father of three children to his books.